Servant Leadership
in the Boardroom:
Fulfilling the Public Trust

By Kent M. Keith

Servant Leadership in the Boardroom: Fulfilling the Public Trust
© Copyright Greenleaf Center for Servant Leadership 2011
Reprinted January 2017

ISBN 13: 978-1-944338-06-0

Published by the Greenleaf Center for Servant Leadership
133 Peachtree St. NE, Lobby Suite 350
Atlanta, GA 30303
www.greenleaf.org

Printed in the United States of America.

Book and cover design by Joe Hunt

SERVANT LEADERSHIP
IN THE
BOARDROOM

FULFILLING THE PUBLIC TRUST

KENT M. KEITH

THE GREENLEAF CENTER FOR SERVANT LEADERSHIP

Contents

Preface VII

Chapter 1: Introduction. 1

Chapter 2: The Public Purpose of Corporctions 6

Chapter 3: Trustees for the Public Good. 14

Chapter 4: The Role of the Board. 23

Chapter 5: The Board and the Administra-ion 35

Chapter 6: The Effective Board 48

Chapter 7: The Call to Serve. 64

Appendix: 67

      Key Reminders for Servant-Leaders in the Boardroom 67

      The Shareholder Primacy Issue 69

      An Overview of Servant Leadership 85

Bibliography. 91

Notes 96

Acknowledgments 105

About the Author 105

About the Greenleaf Center for Servant Leadership 107

Servant Leadership Publications 108

Preface

Corporations, for-profit and non-profit, have an enormous impact on the quality of our daily lives and the character of our society. Corporations are governed by boards. If the boards consisted of servant-leaders, they could raise the performance of their organizations as servant-institutions, and change the world for the better—for all of us. The potential is huge.

The rise of for-profit corporations over the past fifty years has been dramatic. In their book, *The Company*, Micklethwait and Wooldridge argue that the for-profit corporation is so important that today, the basic unit of modern society is not the state, or the political party, or the church. "The most important organization in the world is the company: the basis of the prosperity of the West and the best hope for the future of the rest of the world."[1] They note that using a measure for value added, 37 multinational corporations ranked among the 100 biggest economies in the world in the year 2000, outranking the economies of many countries.[2]

The United States is still a small-business nation. Ninety-nine percent of all the businesses in our country employ fewer than 500 people. These small businesses are important, because they account for 52 percent of all workers. The other 48 percent of all workers are employed by the one percent of the businesses that employ 500 people or more.[3] The impact of these big businesses is obvious. For example, it has been estimated that the Fortune 1,000 companies control about 70 percent of the American economy.[4] The twenty most profitable companies in the United States recorded combined *profits* of $226 billion in 2009. That $226 billion was greater than the gross national products of 150 countries. The $19.3 billion in profit earned by ExxonMobil alone was greater than the gross national products of 110 countries.[5]

The non-profit sector has also grown in importance. As of 2005, a total of 12.9 million people, or 9.7 percent of the nation's workforce, were employed by non-profits.[6] Approximately 1.4 million non-profit organizations were registered with the IRS, an increase of 300,000 during the previous ten years. The revenues of non-profits totaled $1.6 billion and their assets totaled $3.4 trillion, double the revenues and assets recorded ten years earlier. It is estimated that in 2006, a total of 61.2 million Americans— 26.7% of the nation's adult population— volunteered at non-profit organizations. They donated 12.9 billion hours of work.[7]

The dominance of corporations is so complete that it is taken for granted. What is often forgotten is that all corporations are created with government approval, and are given special privileges that are meant to benefit the public. The boards of corporations have the legal authority and responsibility to fulfill that public trust.

Building an effective board is a challenge, but it is a challenge that servant-leaders can meet. Robert K. Greenleaf launched the modern servant leadership movement in 1970 with the publication of his classic essay, *The Servant as Leader*. It was in that essay that he coined the words "servant-leader" and "servant leadership." Greenleaf said that servant-leaders "make sure that other people's highest priority needs are being served."[8] Servant-leaders in the boardroom will focus on the needs of whomever the organization serves— customers, clients, patients, members, students, or citizens. Servant-leaders in the boardroom will also pay attention to the impact the organization is having on its employees, business partners, shareholders or members, and communities. Respecting and responding to the needs of all stakeholders is a challenge, but it is the foundation for efficient, high-performance organizations that truly improve the quality of our lives.[9] (An overview of servant leadership can be found in the Appendix.)

The purpose of this book is to encourage servant-leaders to join boards, and to encourage board members to be servant-leaders, working effectively to fulfill the public trust. The book will present and augment the views of Robert Greenleaf on board members as servant-leaders. It will address both for-profit and non-profit boards, because the origins of all corporations and the roles of their boards are very similar, and Greenleaf's essays addressed both. Also, the differences between the governance of for-profit and non-profit corporations are shrinking. One issue that is different, the assumed primacy of shareholders in a for-profit corporation, is addressed in the Appendix. The discussion will suggest that "board primacy" has overtaken "shareholder primacy" in state law, court decisions, and daily corporate decision-making. Boards can consider all stakeholders, not just shareholders, when they make decisions.

The book begins with background on the public purpose of organizations, the history of corporations, and the responsibility of board members to serve as trustees for the public good. This is followed by a review of the legal power of boards, the advantages of giving that legal power to boards, and the value of board judgments. Then the relationship between boards and administrations is explored, as well as ways to make boards more effective. The book concludes with a call to serve.

There have been too many tragedies—too many cases in which corporations have harmed individuals and communities because their boards did not lead, or their leadership did not fulfill the public trust. Servant leadership in the boardroom can reduce those tragedies, while better aligning corporations with the needs of those they serve. It will never be easy, but dedicated servant-leaders in the boardroom can surely make the world a better place.

K.M.K.

February 2011

1.

Introduction

Robert K. Greenleaf cared deeply about boards. He wrote about them in all four of his major essays, one of which—*Trustees as Servants*—was devoted entirely to boards. He saw the potential for board members to lead their organizations to greater distinction and greater service to society. He wrote in the 1970s, when few people paid any serious attention to boards. That has changed. Today, many people are paying attention, and Greenleaf's ideas are even more timely and relevant than they were before.

As a student at Carleton College in the 1920s, Greenleaf took a course from Dr. Oscar Helming, Chairman of the Economics Department. Helming said something that changed Greenleaf's life. Greenleaf recalled:

> One day, in the course of a rambling lecture, he made a statement like this: 'We are becoming a nation of large institutions...
> Everything is getting big—government, churches, businesses, labor unions, universities—and none of these big institutions are serving well, either the people whom they are set up to serve or the people who staff them to render the service...These institutions can be bludgeoned, coerced, threatened from the outside. But they can only be changed from the inside by somebody who knows how to do it *and who wants to do it.* Some of you folks ought to make your careers inside these institutions and become the ones who respond to the idea that they could do better.'[10]

Greenleaf took Dr. Helming's advice. In 1926 he joined AT&T, which was one of the largest corporations in the world at the time. His thirty-eight years of experience at AT&T convinced him of the importance of major

1

institutions in shaping the quality and character of our daily lives.

Greenleaf knew that our world would be a better place if our institutions were servant-institutions, concerned about how they affect everyone they touch—employees, customers, business partners, shareholders or members, and communities. He saw the need to challenge our institutions to perform at their highest levels of excellence. He said:

> Whereas, until recently, caring was largely person to person, now most of it is mediated through institutions—often large, complex, powerful, impersonal; not always competent; sometimes corrupt. If a better society is to be built, one that is more just and more loving, one that provides greater creative opportunity for its people, then the most open course is to *raise both the capacity to serve and the very performance as servant* of existing major institutions by new regenerative forces operating within them.[11]

Boards can be among the new regenerative forces operating within institutions. If we want to improve the quality of our corporations, we must improve the performance of their boards. Greenleaf said:

> The premise…is that the best of our voluntary (nongovernmental) institutions, in the service of all of us who depend on them, is too far below what is reasonable and possible with their available resources, human and material. This performance can be raised much closer to the optimal for each institution by governing boards of trustees (including directors of business corporations as trustees) who are determined and who organize themselves to do it.[12]

Greenleaf saw board members as "holding prime roles of leadership and influence on which the quality of the total society rests."[13] He knew, however, that boards were not fulfilling their potential for service to their organizations or society. He wrote:

> A basic conceptual flaw in the conventional wisdom of institutional structures is the inadequacy—or even absence—of provision for trustees to be a functioning part of the institution's leadership.

The role of administrators, as it is commonly established, does not provide for adequate trustee functions. Trustees, for their part, have not seen fit to question the assumptions which administrators make and to assert the affirmative and, in the long run, determining role for themselves which is required both by their legal obligations and by the socio-ethical burden of public trust which they carry.[14]

Many boards are not accustomed to leading. They are accustomed to approving whatever the organization's administration recommends. They are nominal, almost honorary boards, playing a ceremonial role. They simply provide the legal window-dressing required for major corporate decisions. Other boards perform only minimal fiduciary duties, and fail to provide true leadership.

Weak and ineffective boards have allowed their institutions to languish or go astray, with very negative impacts on employees, customers, business partners, shareholders or members, communities, the economy, and the environment. Greenleaf did not urge more government regulation as the solution to the problem. He noted:

> Unfortunately, government is expected to provide most of the attention that would enlarge the good and reduce the harm in institutional structures. But government has accepted competition, in the for profit realm, as the prime regulator and builder when, in fact, it may also be the great destroyer of people and the creator of abuses.[15]

Instead of relying on government regulation, Greenleaf urged boards to assume the leadership that they were created to provide. If boards would step *up*, then government regulators would not have to step *in*.

Board members are holders of the charter of public trust for their organizations. They have the legal power to manage the organization. They provide "trustee judgments" that administrators cannot provide, because board members have the perspective of detachment, have their own sources of information, are free from the day-to-day pressure of operations, do not have a career stake in the institution, and are better able to stay focused on the vision and purpose of the organization.

Greenleaf urged boards to truly lead. They should set the goals and define the obligations of the organization. Boards should define where the organization needs to go, and whom it should serve, and how those served—as well as society at large—will benefit from the organization's service. Greenleaf saw the board as a team of equals, with the chair serving as *primus inter pares* or first among equals, responsible to the other board members. Since the role of the board and the role of the administration are different, the chair should not be the CEO. In large organizations, the chair should be half-time or even full-time.

Greenleaf agreed that boards should make policy and administrations should implement those policies. However, his focus was on leadership, and he believed that leadership should be provided by everyone—trustees, administrators, and staff. He recommended that board members help administrators understand how well they are doing, and that board members make sure that leaders are being developed in the organization.

As a result of his many years of experience at AT&T, Greenleaf knew that many ambiguities exist in organizations. It is necessary to be both dogmatic and open to change—dogmatic, so people will know what to do, and open to change, so that new opportunities can be seized. He knew that people who are good at what they do may not be good at examining their operating assumptions. He also understood the necessary tension between belief and criticism. Administrators need to believe in their work in order to get it done, but board members need to be critical, to make sure the work that is being done is the right work.

It was important to Greenleaf that boards get the information they need to perform well. He said that in a large organization, getting the needed information may require the board to hire a permanent, independent staff, as well as consultants reporting directly to the board. Greenleaf also recommended that the board receive continuous coaching. The coach would help the board learn appropriate processes, and facilitate consensus, so the board can achieve one mind and speak with one voice.

But of all the things that board members need to do, Greenleaf emphasized one in particular: They need to *care*. If they care, they will commit their time and energy, and their boards and organizations will truly move forward.

To fully understand Greenleaf's views, we need to go back in time. We turn now to the first corporations, and the public purposes for which they were created.

2.

The Public Purpose of Corporations

Why do organizations exist? They exist to meet people's needs. Since time immemorial, people have come together to achieve as groups the things that they cannot achieve as individuals. In prehistoric times they came together to hunt, or for mutual protection from predators; later, to farm, and to create and trade goods. They formed governments to lead their tribes, then their kingdoms, city-states, and nations. As societies and their economies became more complex, so did organizations. By the nineteenth century, the establishment of bureaucracies was considered to be an important step forward, because bureaucracies sought to rationalize and formalize communications within increasingly complex organizations. Today it is nearly impossible to do anything entirely by oneself, without relying on one or more organizations.

Although organizations are now very complex, they still exist to meet people's needs. That is true whether the organization is public, private, non-profit, or academic. Organizations obtain income in different ways—from sales, fees, donations, or tax revenues—but each organization exists to serve customers, clients, patients, students, members, participants, or citizens.

There are those in the private sector who think that their businesses exist to make money—to make a profit. But that confuses a need with a purpose. If the purpose of a business is to make money, then by analogy the purpose of a government is to collect taxes, the purpose of a university is to collect tuition, and the purpose of a non-profit organization is to collect donations and fees. Certainly, all organizations need to obtain resources, but that is not their purpose. Their purpose is to serve their customers, clients, patients, students, members, participants, or citizens. *Organizations don't exist to make money, they make money so they can continue to exist.* They make money so they can continue to grow in service to others. Their purpose is to make life better for those they serve. Their purpose is to change lives, even save lives, through the programs, products, and services that they provide.

Of course, organizations cannot meet the needs of customers without meeting the needs of their employees, colleagues, or associates who actually provide the programs, products, or services. Employees need the skills, equipment, and time to serve customers well. They need to earn a fair wage, so they can take care of themselves and their families. They also need meaning and purpose in their lives.

Fortunately, meaning and purpose are readily available. After all, when people go to work each day, they go to work to meet the needs of others. They help others to get food, clothing, shelter, healthcare, education, and recreation. Meeting the needs of others is a meaningful, even noble activity. It can be seen as a calling. Each of us can find deep satisfaction from knowing that when we go to work each day, we get what *we* need by helping other people to get what *they* need. We do that by serving others through our organizations.

The first corporations and their public purposes

Corporations as we know them today are a comparatively new phenomenon in the history of organizations. The word "corporation" comes from the Latin word "corporare," which means "to form into a body." In medieval Europe, churches and local governments were often incorporated. Governments gave them charters that allowed them to continue beyond the lives of their individual members.

Centuries ago, when governments identified a public need, they often granted a corporate charter to a group of private citizens who then invested their money to meet that need. The charters could be revoked if the public purpose was not met. For example, early corporations in Europe were not-for-profit organizations that built hospitals and universities. The constitutions of these organizations detailed their duties, which were overseen by the government. Stepping beyond the specific duties in the charter was punishable by law.

Governments chartered profit-making corporations in the seventeenth century to finance their expansion overseas and control trade and resources in Asia, Africa, and America. These "chartered companies" included the Hudson's Bay Company, the Dutch East India Company, and the British East India Company. Merchants invested their funds in the company and created a commercial corporation with the powers of a government. At its height in the early nineteenth century, the British East India Company controlled India, monopolizing trade and ruling over a fifth of the world's population. The company had a private army of a quarter of a million soldiers. It was not until 1858 that the British government eliminated the East India Company's territorial powers.

British corporations also exercised monopolistic powers in the American colonies. The corporations shipped raw materials from the colonies to Britain for manufacture, and then sold the finished goods back to the American colonies.

In the first decades after independence, commercial enterprises in the United States were mostly sole proprietorships and partnerships. Adolph A. Berle and Gardiner C. Means, in *The Modern Corporation & Private Property*, pointed out that the small number of corporations that existed in the early years were established for public purposes:

> In 1800 the corporate form was used in America mainly for undertakings involving a direct public interest: the construction of turnpikes, bridges and canals, the operation of banks and insurance companies, and the creation of fire brigades. Up to that year only 335 profit-seeking corporations appear to have been formed in the United States, nearly all incorporated in the last decade of the Eighteenth Century. Of these, 219 were turnpike, bridge and canal companies, and another 36 furnished water and fire protection or dock facilities. Banks and insurance companies had just begun to assume corporate form and numbered 67 at the opening of the century. Manufacturing industry lay almost wholly outside the corporate field, being represented by only 6 corporations.[16]

Most early corporations conducted activities that were similar to public utilities and were seen to be of value to the community. The chartering of general business corporations "was justified on the grounds that these corporations served the public interest."[17] The first American treatise on the law of private corporations, published in 1832, declared that "the design of a corporation is to provide for some good that is useful to the public," and that "nearly every corporation is public, inasmuch as they are created for the public benefit."[18]

During the early nineteenth century, state governments paid a lot of attention to the granting of corporate charters. Forming a corporation required an act of the state legislature, and few charters were granted. The chartering process often involved a lot of public debate. The charters that were granted were usually for public functions such as digging canals, and building roads and bridges.

The corporations that were chartered by state governments could only engage in the specific activities for which they were chartered. The charters included detailed operating conditions, which were echoed in state laws and even state constitutions.

> ...State legislatures inserted regulatory provisions into corporate charters and...also routinely added clauses that allowed the state to alter unilaterally a charter's terms. Regulatory provisions ranged from restrictions on the amount of capital that firms could raise and the lines of business in which they could engage to requirements that specific types of corporations, for example banks, submit semi-annual reports. Legislatures also imposed particular structures of governance on corporate enterprises, specifying, for example, the size and composition of boards of directors, the frequency of elections for corporate officers, and the number of votes that large shareholders could exercise.[19]

Corporations could be terminated if they exceeded their charters, caused public harm, or acted illegally. The government granted charters that were limited in time, usually between ten and forty years. If the legislature did not renew the charter, the corporation was dissolved, and the assets were divided among shareholders. Some charters required the dissolution of a corporation when it completed the task for which it was chartered. According to Micklethwait and Wooldridge, "as late as 1903, almost half the states limited the duration of corporate charters to between twenty and fifty years. Throughout the nineteenth century, legislatures revoked charters when the corporation wasn't deemed to be fulfilling its responsibilities."[20]

Typically, corporate charters prohibited corporations from owning stock in other corporations. They could not own property unless it was essential to their chartered purpose, and they were prohibited from making political contributions.[21] The reason for all these limitations was clear: Corporations were established for a public purpose, and the government maintained close control to make sure the public purpose was fulfilled.

The privileges of the modern corporation

The government role in the granting of corporate charters began to change in the mid-nineteenth century. Between 1830 and 1860 the number of businesses seeking incorporation was so large that state legislatures decided they could no longer make individual grants. States also sought to make incorporation easier, as a way to attract business.[22] They therefore passed general incorporation laws that granted the privilege of incorporation to all applicants who could meet the requirements.[23]

An act passed by the British Parliament in 1844 allowed corporations to incorporate without a royal charter or act of Parliament, and also allowed corporations to define their own purpose. Legislation in 1855 and 1856 granted limited liability to shareholders in a corporation, so that their personal assets were protected in the event that the corporations they owned were sued or went bankrupt.[24] Individual investors were no longer personally liable for the corporation's behavior. Similar provisions were also adopted in the United States.

As a result, the modern corporation is legally separate from the people who created it. If a for-profit corporation fails, shareholders may lose their investment and employees may lose their jobs, but neither the shareholders nor the employees will be liable for the debts of the corporation unless they personally guaranteed them. Similarly, if a not-for-profit corporation fails, employees may lose their jobs, but they are not liable for the debts.

The new legislation had its opponents. It was argued that limited liability was wrong because it was, in effect, a state subsidy.[25] Others pointed out that limited liability simply shifted the risk of doing business from the shareholders and managers of a company to the company's customers, lenders, and suppliers—all of whom could be left with a loss if the company failed and could not pay its creditors.[26] However, limited liability made it much easier for entrepreneurs to obtain capital. They could raise money by issuing shares instead of borrowing from their families, friends, and banks. The economic development advantages were significant, and carried the day.

By the end of the nineteenth century, then, the special privileges of the modern corporation were: (1) it could define its own purpose, (2) it could continue indefinitely without having to renew its charter, and (3) it could operate with limited liability accruing to individual investors or employees. Limited liability was—and still is—an important privilege that is granted to corporations. It is a privilege that is not available to sole proprietorships or most forms of partnerships.

As legislation expanded their privileges, corporations continued to grow in number and influence. They also changed their focus. While corporations began as vehicles for building public projects, by the middle of the nineteenth century they had become vehicles for building private fortunes. The industrial revolution gave rise to factories and company towns, and the Civil War provided opportunities for corporations to amass great wealth. Business expanded dramatically, and huge corporations emerged. As corporations grew stronger, government and court doctrines changed to support them. For example, "in the United States, the law came to view the corporation the same as it would an individual."[27] Corporations were given the same rights as natural persons.

The government's grant of a charter to incorporate an organization was not a mere legal technicality. Looking back on America's economic history, it is clear that the granting of charters was a major policy decision. According to the *Encyclopedia of American Economic History*:

The power to issue charters of incorporation to business entrepreneurs was of supreme importance... Laws providing for incorporation, and for the conditions under which private enterprise could operate, have had a far-reaching impact on the economic structure of the nation.[28]

The blurring of corporate types

Today, the two most common types of corporations are for-profit corporations that distribute a portion of their profits to shareholders, and non-profit corporations that reinvest surpluses in their charitable or membership activities.

However, in recent years the distinctions between these two types of corporation have begun to blur. Non-profits that once depended almost entirely on donations have begun to rely on fees for service, and have created businesses to supplement their income. Bill Shore, in *The Cathedral Within*, described non-profit organizations that established businesses to create jobs for the people they wished to assist, such as the poor, the disabled, or former prisoners who needed jobs so they could start a new life.[29]

Meanwhile, some corporations classified as "for-profit" corporations have become "social businesses." Muhammad Yunus launched the modern micro-credit revolution by making small loans and starting social businesses in Bangladesh. In his book, *Creating a World Without Poverty*, Yunus argued that "we need a new type of business that pursues goals other than making personal profit—a business that is totally dedicated to solving social and environmental problems."[30] Such a business is like a profit-maximizing business in that it employs workers, creates goods and services, sells its goods and services to customers, and collects revenue. But, as Yunus pointed out:

> ...its underlying objective—and the criterion by which it should be evaluated—is to create social benefits for those whose lives it touches... A social business is a company that is cause-driven rather than profit-driven, with the potential to act as a change agent for the world."[31]

For example, a social business could sell high-quality food products at low prices to meet the nutritional needs of poor children, or it could develop renewable energy systems and sell them at low prices to rural communities that have no energy supply. Profits are used to pay back investors and to grow the business.

While the lines between for-profit and non-profit organizations have begun to blur, one simple fact remains clear: All corporations are chartered and given special privileges by the government in order to achieve the greater public good. That good may be in the form of the charitable and educational work performed by a non-profit; or the investment, technological innovation, and jobs created by a for-profit corporation; or the business activities of a non-profit; or the public purposes fulfilled by a social business. Whatever the case, the privileges of incorporation are granted by the government for the public good.

3.

Trustees for the Public Good

Legislatures long ago ceased debating the charter of each new corporation to determine its public purpose and the public benefits. But legislatures were clear about who was to exercise responsibility for fulfilling the public good. They put that responsibility in the hands of board members.

Greenleaf understood this responsibility of board members as a form of trusteeship. He said:

> *Trusteeship* is the holding of a charter of public trust *for* an institution. As the term is understood here, it represents a function carried out through membership on the governing board of an incorporated institution and is defined by law...[32]

> Trustees are accountable to all parties at interest for the best possible performance of the institution in the service of the needs of all constituencies—including society at large.[33]

Boards are found in three major sectors: government agencies, non-profit organizations, and for-profit corporations. Regardless of which sector they operate in, boards hold the charter of public trust for the organization.

This is easy to understand in the case of a government board that has a defined public clientele—a city, a school district, or citizens with specific needs. The government board is clearly called to serve the public. It is also easy to understand in the case of non-profit organizations, which include social service organizations, educational institutions, hospitals, churches, and museums. They are focused on serving members of the public, or their own members, to achieve the greater public good. In recognition of their public purposes, non-profit organizations can be granted tax-exempt status by the government.

It is more unusual to argue that the boards of for-profit business organizations hold a charter of public trust for their organizations. But that was true of the early corporations, and Greenleaf believed it should be true of for-profit corporations today.

Greenleaf worked for AT&T for thirty-eight years. He was a businessman. He believed that a business needs to make a profit. But he also believed that a business, along with all other organizations, needs to be a servant-institution that cares about all the people that the organization touches—employees, customers, business partners, shareholders, and communities.

Some economists argue that the primary purpose of a for-profit organization is to maximize shareholder value. The reason, they say, is that the shareholders are the owners. However, the simple fact is that shareholders do not own the corporation, they own shares.[34] As owners of shares, they have the right to vote for members of the board, the right to share in corporate earnings when dividends are declared by the board, and the right to a share of the assets of the corporation if any are available when the corporation dissolves. However, these rights are very limited.[35]

Furthermore, there are problems with the "shareholder primacy" view, since it can be used to justify the exploitation of employees, customers, business partners, communities, and the environment, all in the name of maximizing returns to shareholders. Legislatures and courts today support the right of boards of directors to consider the impacts of their decisions on *all* stakeholders, not just shareholders. The boards of for-profit corporations can exercise their charter of public trust on behalf of everyone that the corporation touches. (A more complete discussion of the shareholder primacy issue can be found in the Appendix.)

Boards have the legal responsibility to manage the organization

When state legislatures gave boards the responsibility for the public good, they gave boards the legal power to achieve that public good. Boards have the legal power to manage the organization.

"Inherent in the concept of the corporation is the fact that individuals can form a corporation only with the legal permission of government."[36] As the American Bar Association notes, "corporations do not exist simply by mutual agreement of members or directors but come into being only by a specific act of a state or federal government and are kept in existence only by compliance with the regular requirements of that government." [37]

The requirements for incorporation are minimal. Permission to form a corporation can be obtained by filing a charter of incorporation with the appropriate state agency. Usually, the charter need only give the corporation's name and mailing address, purpose, and the names and addresses of three individuals who will serve as the incorporators, one of whom must live in the state.

Charters assign all the powers, duties, and responsibilities of the corporation to the board, which is most often known as a "board of directors," but can also have other names, such as "board of trustees," "board of governors," "board of regents," or "board of overseers." Section 8 of the Model Business Corporation Act provides that "each corporation must have a board of directors," and "all corporate powers shall be exercised by or under the authority of, and the business and affairs of the corporation managed by or under the direction of, its board of directors…"[38] Any exceptions require a special agreement among the shareholders.

While non-profit organizations differ from for-profit corporations, the American Bar Association Committee on Nonprofit Corporations states:

> The rights and duties of directors of nonprofit corporations are in many respects similar to those imposed on directors of for-profit or business corporations. In a large number of states, the statute

governing nonprofit corporations has been modeled at least to some degree on the statute governing for-profit corporations.[39]

The legal power of the board to manage the corporation is clearly stated in corporation documents. For example, the following language is typical of corporate bylaws:

> All of the authority of the corporation shall be exercised by or under the direction of the board of directors. The board of directors is empowered to adopt rules and regulations for the conduct of their meetings; to appoint or approve the appointment of committees, and to discontinue the same; to define the duties of officers and committees; to employ and define the duties of agents and employees; to delegate duties; to approve budgets and policies for the corporation; to elect a successor to hold office for the unexpired portion of the term of any officer or member of the board of directors whose place shall be vacant at any time; and in general, to exercise and perform all the powers necessary to conduct the work of the corporation.

There is thus no doubt about the board's legal powers. As Greenleaf said:

> Trustees have a kind of power that administrators and staffs do not have—they have the legal power to manage everything in the institution; they have all the legal power there is. They may delegate some of it, but they can also take it back. *They cannot give any of it away, irretrievably, and still be trustees*... The essential definition of the trustee role is that trustees, as a body, hold all of the ultimate (legal) authority.[40]

Having been given power, the board should make sure that it is used for constructive ends. Greenleaf argued that "trustees have the obligation to oversee the use of power in order to check its corrupting influence on those to whom it is entrusted, and to assure that those affected by its use are positively helped and are not harmed."[41] He added:

Trustees delegate the operational use of power to administrators and staffs, but with accountability for its use that is at least as strict as now obtains with the use of property and money. Furthermore, trustees will insist that the outcome be that people in, and affected by, the institution will grow healthier, wiser, freer, more autonomous, and more likely to become servants of society.[42]

Why boards instead of individual leaders?

Did legislatures make the right decision when they decided to put all the power in the hands of boards instead of individuals? There are at least four reasons to believe that their decision was a wise one: (1) manageability, (2) accountability, (3) avoiding the corruptive influence of concentrated power, and (4) better decisions.

Manageability. For-profit corporations have many shareholders, non-profit corporations have many members, and government agencies have many citizens in their jurisdictions. Asking the shareholders, members, or citizens to directly manage their organizations is not realistic. There are too many people, they have a variety of potentially conflicting interests, and it would be difficult to get them all together on a regular basis to make decisions. The decision-making function needs to be centralized if it is to be manageable. Boards achieve that centralization.

Accountability. Boards are a better choice than a single individual, because shareholders, members, or citizens would find it too difficult to be sufficiently informed to effectively monitor a single decision-maker's performance. If all the power were in the hands of an individual, the individual would, for all practical purposes, be accountable to no one. The advantage of a board is that its members can hold *each other* accountable.

Avoiding the corruptive influence of concentrated power. Greenleaf quoted Lord Acton's maxim that "power tends to corrupt and absolute power corrupts absolutely."[43] Greenleaf was very concerned about the temptations of unrestrained individual power. An individual who is given power may not be able to resist the temptation to *rule* rather than to *serve*. Those who operate with few limits on their power may end up harming or destroying their organizations while pursuing their personal agendas. Greenleaf concluded that "*no one, absolutely no one, is to be entrusted with the operational use of power without the close oversight of fully functioning trustees.*"[44]

As William G. Bowen wrote in *The Board Book*:

> Both for-profit and non-profit entities operate in inherently complex settings in which matters are rarely cut-and-dried. The exercise of collective responsibility through the mechanism of the board can slow down decision making, but it can also dampen the enthusiasm of the aspiring autocrat. A properly functioning board provides checks and balances by adding layers of judgment and protections against the abuse of power, self-dealing, favoritism, and just plain foolishness.[45]

Better decisions. Putting the power in the hands of a group is also the best way to get effective decisions for the good of the organization. According to Stephen Bainbridge in *The New Corporate Governance in Theory and Practice*: "Groups turn out to have significant advantages vis-à-vis individuals at exercising critical evaluative judgment, which is precisely the principal skill set needed at the top of the corporate hierarchy."[46] As Richard Chait, Thomas Holland, and Barbara Taylor put it, one of the reasons for empowering a board is that "properly constituted and engaged, the group will make better decisions than individuals or a subgroup."[47] This was the conclusion of a study conducted by Larry Michaelsen, Warren Watson, and Robert Black involving 1,334 students, during which the researchers tested them as individuals and then in groups on a variety of decision-making tasks. The result was that 215 of the 222 groups (97%) outperformed their best member.[48] As the saying goes, more heads are better than one.

From the managerial age to board primacy

The beginning of the 20th century marked the rise of professional managers, leading ever-larger and more complex corporations. The result has been called "managerial capitalism." According to Bainbridge:

> Managerial capitalism reached its high-water mark in the 1950s. The boards of this era were largely 'an extension of management.' Eight out of ten directors in this period were either employees

(insiders) or outsiders closely affiliated with the corporation, such as the firm's lawyers and bankers. The boards of this era saw their function mainly as advisory rather than as being comprised of either management or monitoring. Their low compensation and modest stock ownership (if any) combined with strong 'don't rock the boat' social norms ensured that most boards were passive.[49]

Peter Drucker wrote:

> In a good many businesses, especially in large publicly held ones, boards have become slumber parties. They only wake up when there is a serious crisis and usually when it is way too late. In the large and successful petroleum companies that grew out of Rockefeller's Standard Oil Trust, but also in companies in Europe and Japan, boards have traditionally been a legal fiction. Some nonprofits, too—large private universities or large churches dominated by a powerful, charismatic pastor—have reduced their boards to a purely ceremonial role.[50]

The emphasis on the CEO led many CEOs of for-profit corporations to assume the role of board chair. The Chairman/CEO could pick friends and allies to be board members, thus further concentrating his or her control over the corporation. For a few, the temptation to abuse this power was overwhelming, with scandalous and even tragic results.

The climate began to change in the 1960s and 1970s, when reformers and social activists criticized antisocial corporate behaviors such as environmental pollution, discrimination, dangerous workplaces, and unsafe products. They called for greater accountability to the public.

It was in the 1970s that Greenleaf began writing his essays on servant leadership and trustees. While there was greater public focus during this period on the need for better corporate behavior, the focus was not on boards. When attention was given to boards, it was in the context of the failure of for-profit corporations to be accountable to their shareholders. A "monitoring model" emerged, in which boards were called upon to evaluate the performance of the corporation's management. It was argued that a majority of the board members should be independent, and should be able to get assistance from corporate employees, hire experts to advise the board on special issues, and inspect corporate records and interview corporate employees without having to go through the senior executives.[51] The "monitoring model" was focused on the management performance of senior executives, not leadership by the board.

Interest in the role of the corporate board continued to grow. For example, in 1978, an American Bar Association Committee on Corporate Laws produced the *Corporate Director's Guidebook*, and in 1990, John Carver published his first book on his Policy Governance® Model. Statements of "best practices" emerged, often in very detailed forms.

The corporate scandals at Enron, WorldCom, Tyco, HealthSouth, Adelphia, and other for-profit corporations led to the Sarbanes-Oxley Act of 2002, also known as SOX. The new legislation mandated changes in corporate practices, including board practices, in order to protect shareholders and the general public from accounting errors and fraud. Some of those practices have been adopted by the boards of non-profit organizations as well, often as a result of new requirements passed by state legislatures.

According to Bainbridge, "although the SOX reforms covered virtually the entire corporate governance waterfront, it's fair to say that empowering boards of directors and insisting that they become more effective were key major goals."[52] Much of the focus was on audit committees, due to the recent scandals. However, reforms were enacted by the stock exchanges, which amended their listing requirements in order to:

- Require that a majority of the members of the board of directors of most listed companies must be independent of management
- Define independence using very strict bright-line rules [clear written rules that state what is legal and illegal in specific situations as opposed to rules based on case law and precedent]
- Expand the duties and powers of the independent directors
- Expand the duties and powers of the audit committee of the board of directors.[53]

The impact of SOX has been significant:

> Boards of directors can no longer act as passive advisors for the
> CEOs who have handpicked them, often in an effort to keep control
> of the company. Members of corporate boards must take an
> increasingly active role in fulfilling their fiduciary responsibilities of
> oversight. They are no longer 'window dressing,' and they should
> act effectively to add value to the company.[54]

Ram Charan wrote in *Boards that Deliver:*

> Boards of directors have undergone a rapid transformation since
> the Sarbanes-Oxley Act of 2002. The shift in power between
> the CEO and the board is perceptible. Directors are taking their
> responsibilities seriously, speaking up, and taking action. It's a
> positive trend and an exciting time for boards.[55]

In addition to the shift in power between the CEO and the board,
state legislatures and courts have made it clear that boards have the legal
authority to address the needs of all stakeholders of a for-profit corporation,
not just shareholders. There has been a shift from "shareholder primacy" to
"board primacy."

Many of these changes were consistent with the recommendations that
Greenleaf made thirty years earlier. His views turned out to be prophetic. It
would be fair to say that "before there was Sarbanes-Oxley, there was Robert
Greenleaf." He urged the board to work with but be independent of the
organization's administration; to separate the chair and CEO roles; and to
develop the board's own sources of information. He sought a true leadership
role for boards. He called on them to provide board judgments and set goals
that add value to their organizations. And he urged corporations to serve all
of their stakeholders—employees, customers, business partners, shareholders
or members, and communities.

4.

The Role of the Board

Responsibilities and functions of the board

In *The Board Book*, Bowen said that "at the most general level, all boards can be said to share a single over-arching responsibility: *to build an effective organization*. Everything else is derivative."[56]

Robert Greenleaf believed that the board could build an effective organization if it would initiate and lead, instead of just reacting. Boards should not be nominal or honorary boards. They should not just approve administration recommendations. They should be thought leaders.

Board members should set the context for those who are operating the organization. They should provide the big picture, the larger context, for the organization's work. The board should stay in touch with social, economic, environmental, and political trends that can affect the organization.

Board members should be servant-leaders, concerned with the ways in which the organization serves all the people it touches. As John Carver says, "proper governance is a logical impossibility if it does not include the concept of servant leadership."[57]

Greenleaf said that the major trustee functions are:

> a. *To set the goals, to define the obligations and the general premises—or the concept—of the institution, and to approve plans for reaching goals.* All of the parties at interest should be consulted, and administrative and professional staffs should be listened to most carefully. However,

the established goals are the trustees' own goals. Ideas may come from any source, but goals are trustee formulated, not just trustee approved or trustee affirmed.

b. *To appoint the top administrative officers, to design the top administrative structure, to design and assign the duties of individuals in that group, and to act so as to motivate administrators and professionals.* Trustees do not rubber-stamp administrative recommendations on these matters.

c. *To assess, at appropriate times, the performance of the institution,* its major parts, and the work of its top executives in the pursuit of the established goals.

d. *To take appropriate action* based on what is found in the above assessment.[58]

Other writers describe board responsibilities in similar terms. For example, Bowen argued that all boards have eight principal functions:

1. Select, encourage, advise, evaluate, compensate, and, if need be, replace the CEO.
2. Discuss, review, and approve strategic directions.
3. Monitor performance.
4. Ensure that the organization operates responsibly as well as effectively.
5. Act on specific policy recommendations and mobilize support for decisions taken.
6. Provide a buffer for the president or CEO—in the vernacular, 'take some of the heat.'
7. Ensure that the necessary resources, both human and financial, will be available to pursue the organization's strategies and achieve its objectives.
8. Nominate suitable candidates for election to the board, and establish and carry out an effective system of governance at the board level.[59]

Richard T. Ingram, in *Ten Basic Responsibilities of Nonprofit Boards*, provided the following list:

1. *Determine mission and purpose.* It is the board's responsibility to create and review a statement of mission and purpose that articulates the organization's goals, means, and primary constituents served.
2. *Select the chief executive.* Boards must reach consensus on the chief executive's responsibilities and undertake a careful search to find the most qualified individual for the position.
3. *Support and evaluate the chief executive.* The board should ensure that the chief executive has the moral and professional support he or she needs to further the goals of the organization.
4. *Ensure effective planning.* Boards must actively participate in an overall planning process and assist in implementing and monitoring the plan's goals.
5. *Monitor and strengthen programs and services.* The board's responsibility is to determine which programs are consistent with the organization's mission and monitor their effectiveness.
6. *Ensure adequate financial resources.* One of the board's foremost responsibilities is to secure adequate resources for the organization to fulfill its mission.
7. *Protect assets and provide proper financial oversight.* The board must assist in developing the annual budget and ensuring that proper financial controls are in place.
8. *Build a competent board.* All boards have a responsibility to articulate prerequisites for candidates, orient new members, and periodically and comprehensively evaluate their own performance.
9. *Ensure legal and ethical integrity.* The board is ultimately responsible for adherence to legal standards and ethical norms.
10. *Enhance the organization's public standing.* The board should clearly articulate the organization's mission, accomplishments, and goals to the public and garner support from the community.[60]

Non-profit organizations are typically focused on their mission, which board members are expected to champion. For example, in orienting new board members, the YMCA of Honolulu included these responsibilities: (1) Believe in YMCA goals and work with staff as partners in serving the community; (2) Understand the YMCA—its purpose, goals, programs, and methods; (3) Interpret the YMCA to the community, be a YMCA spokesperson, and represent the YMCA in the community; (4) Solicit funds, participate in fund-raising campaigns, open doors for others to raise funds and contribute within one's own means; and (5) Help recruit new volunteers and members.[61]

David Hubbard, President of Fuller Theological Seminary, described how he saw the functions of the board of his organization:

> Board members are governors. When they sit around the table and vote their 'I so move,' they govern the institution. Board members are sponsors, and here we get to their role in giving money and raising money. They are ambassadors—interpreting the mission of the institution, defending it when it's under pressure, representing it in their constituencies and communities. Finally, they are consultants; almost every trustee will have some professional skill which would be expensive if you had to buy it… Governor, sponsor, ambassador, and consultant would be the four major roles.[62]

In regard to trustees as consultants, Greenleaf would warn that the board should not delegate certain topics to specific board members, even if they are experts on those topics. Advice is welcomed, but all issues belong to the full board, not just one member.

Goal setting is a key responsibility of the board. Greenleaf said:

> The first thing an institution needs to do in order to start on a conspicuously higher course is to state clearly where it wants to go, whom it wants to serve, and how it expects those served directly, as well as society at large, to benefit from the service. Unless these are clearly understood, an institution cannot approach its optimum performance.[63]

John and Miriam Carver stated that board decisions should

predominantly be policy decisions, based on values the board develops as its own. The Carvers believe that all policies should fall into four categories: (1) ends, which refer to what results are to be achieved, for whom, and at what cost; (2) executive limitations, which refer to the boundaries of acceptability within which staff members can make their own decisions; (3) board-staff linkage, which refers to the manner in which the board delegates authority to the staff and how it evaluates staff performance; and (4) the governance process, which refers to the board philosophy and how the board does its work.[64]

The Carvers see the determination of ends as the pivotal duty of governance. They said: "The ends of an organization are the reasons for its existence. It is obvious that careful, wise selection of ends is the highest calling of trustee leadership."[65] Board members should not simply review staff decisions or recommendations, but act more as a think tank, focused on organizational outcomes. "Ends language is never about what the organization will be doing; it is always about what will be different for others."[66]

David H. Smith in *Entrusted: The Moral Responsibilities of Trusteeship*, described three principles that should guide the work of a board: the fiduciary principle, the common good principle, and the obligation to act as a community of interpretation. He said that trustees must be loyal to the purpose for which the organization was created, and trustees must use moral means to achieve morally worthy ends. In regard to a acting as a community of interpretation, Smith wrote:

> A board of trustees must be able to interpret an institution's history in order to reconcile its essential distinctive vision with the overall good of society. The trustees must be able to select from the past so as to plan for the future... The board's major role is reflective: Its major moral responsibility is to establish the identity or vocation of the organization.[67]

In their book *Governance as Leadership: Reframing the Work of Nonprofit Boards*, Richard P. Chait, William P. Ryan, and Barbara E. Taylor argued that a board must govern in three modes: fiduciary, strategic, and generative. In the fiduciary mode, a board seeks to monitor the use of resources, assures that the organization remains faithful to its mission, and makes sure that trustees govern in the best interests of the organization. This mode addresses the board's duties of loyalty and care, which are "the fundamental work of trusteeship."[68]

In the strategic mode, "an organization seeks to align internal strengths and weaknesses with external opportunities and threats, all in pursuit of organizational impact."[69] The role of the board shifts from oversight to ideas about the organization's future.

While the first two modes are important, Chait and his colleagues believe that it is in the third mode, the generative mode, that boards can make their biggest contributions, because the generative mode is "the most fertile soil for boards to flower as a source of leadership."[70] It is in this mode that insight, wisdom, and creativity are brought to bear in ways that can result in paradigm shifts. Generative thinking does not produce knowledge, information, or data, but rather, "generative thinking produces a sense of what knowledge, information, and data *mean.*"[71] It is about sense-making, based on cues and clues, the use of different frames, and thinking about the past in order to project the future. Chait and his colleagues stated:

> As long as governing means what most people think it means—setting the goals and direction of an organization and holding the management accountable for progress toward those goals—then generative thinking has to be essential to governing. Generative thinking is where goal-setting and direction-setting originate. The contributions boards make to mission-setting, strategy-development, and problem solving certainly shape organizations. But it is *cues* and *frames,* along with *retrospective thinking,* that enable the *sense-making* on which these other processes depend.[72]

The uniqueness of board judgments

Greenleaf argued that boards provide something that nobody else in the organization can provide—board judgments. In his essay, *Trustees as Servants,* Greenleaf wrote:

Although trustees may not have professional or administrative expertise in the particular institution, theirs is not a *lay* judgment. It is a unique thing, a *trustee judgment*, and it stands on a par in importance with any other judgment within the institution.[73]

Greenleaf described trustee judgment as follows:

It is a meld of the following unique aspects of the role of trustee: (1) trustees have the perspective of detachment that no insider can have; (2) they have their own information source that equips them for their special functions (3) they are free from the pressures and minutia of day-to-day operations so that they can take an overview as well as project the future; (4) trustees do not have a career stake in the institution—their motivation can be less self-centered; (5) effective trustees stand as symbols of trust; therefore they can provide a shelter of legitimacy in a way that deeply committed insiders cannot; (6) because trustees are not colleagues who may have contending interests they can function creatively as a group on issues that internal constituencies may not be able to resolve; (7) trustees are better able to have a sense of history, past-present-future, and therefore are better able to hold the institution's vision and keep it steady, and they may better see the path to survival and long service; (8) trustees can keep the concept of ultimate purpose in sharp focus and hold it up as a guide at times when the insiders are hard pressed to stay afloat from day to day.[74]

Greenleaf went on to say:

The trustee who has good trustee judgment, and who wants to gain ground in building a better institution, will know that three decisions need to be made about any action that, in the test of time, turns out well: (1) There is a good idea; (2) good people are committed to carrying it out; and (3) authority is placed at their disposal.

A good trustee judgment, one that stands on a par with all other judgments and is respected by all other constituents, is a blend of good judgments on all three of these elements. An error on any one of them will doom the action to failure. Only trustees are in a position to make a good judgment and to set the policies to guide others in making such judgments on *any one* of these elements. Trustees do not have all of the answers, but they can best utilize what data there is in making some crucial judgments and in establishing policies to guide others' judgments.[75]

Board actions must meet three legal standards: the duty of care, the duty of loyalty, and the duty of obedience. The duty of care requires each board member to be prudent, act in good faith, and participate in the governance process. The duty of loyalty requires each board member to be faithful to the organization's priorities, and put the good of the organization ahead of the board member's professional or personal interests. The duty of obedience requires each board member to be faithful to the organization's mission, and comply with applicable laws as well as the organization's bylaws.[76]

The board chair

To be effective, boards need effective chairs. Greenleaf said: "We cannot have better institutions unless we have better leadership in chairmen."[77] He wrote:

> …The chairman, as leader of the trustees, should be selected by his colleagues for his dedication to optimal performance of the institution and for his ability to make the trustee role an exciting, creative, and very responsible endeavor, far more rewarding to the able trustee than the prevailing reactive role. The chairman, thus concerned, would be *primus inter pares*, not chief. He would be a first among equals and responsible to his peers, the trustees.[78]

Max De Pree, in *Called to Serve*, stated that "chairing is where servant leadership comes strongly into play."[79] He described the role of the chair as building trust, drawing out the members, being an aggressive listener, and helping the board to move away from personal agendas so it can focus on the corporate agenda. He said:

…The chairperson must be diligent in saying thank you…The chairperson must be just as diligent in holding the group accountable. By the nature of the chairperson's position, no one else in the group can hold the board accountable if she fails to do it…This is the way in which the chairperson holds the group accountable—by whether or not the group measures up to the goals and standards they have set for themselves…[80]

In preparing for board meetings, the chair works with the administration to make sure that appropriate information is provided to the board in advance so that the board can make the best use of its time during its meetings. In conducting board meetings, the chair is a facilitator, helping board members to understand the agenda, to grasp the ways in which issues relate to each other and to long-term goals, and to recall the milestones that have been achieved. The chair invites discussion without allowing the meeting to wander, and identifies the purpose of each discussion—is it to brainstorm, or give advice to the administration, or make a decision? At the end of each discussion, the chair articulates who is going to do what and by when, so that it is clear who will be following up.[81]

Separating the chair and CEO positions

Greenleaf argued for the separation of the chair and CEO positions. He said: "First and foremost, the trustee chairman will *not* be an officer of administration. In fact, his best career route may not be through administration at all…"[82]

The separation of the chair and CEO positions has been common in non-profit organizations, but it has not been the case in many for-profit corporations. However, the tide is turning. As Bowen said:

The day of the imperial CEO is, and should be, over…the CEO-centric model is unnecessarily risky and suboptimal in other respects. In sum, it deprives the board…of an important protection against abuses of power. In addition, it decreases the likelihood that the CEO (and all board members, for that matter) will hear the kinds of authentic second opinions that should be expressed freely in meetings of a truly engaged, independent board that knows it is accountable and feels comfortable debating key issues.[83]

Bowen cited the arguments in favor of separating the roles in for-profit corporations. The two advantages are that having a separate chairman:

(1) Positions the board to exercise properly its key oversight responsibility vis-à-vis the CEO, reduces the risk of autocratic rule by creating a regime of checks and balances, and promotes a healthy dynamic in board deliberations.
(2) Divides the heavy workload by allowing the CEO to concentrate on managing the business while the chairman concentrates on managing board affairs.[84]

A primary role of the board is to hire, evaluate, and if necessary fire the CEO. There is an obvious conflict of interest when the CEO is the Chair of the board that is supposed to evaluate his or her performance. There is also the problem of concentrating too much power in the hands of a single Chairman/CEO, who may stack the board with friends and allies, further concentrating his or her power. When the roles are separate, the board has an arms-length relationship with the CEO; power is better distributed; and board members are more likely to have open and honest discussions about the management of the organization.

In addition, when the roles are separate, the Chair can help the CEO by addressing board issues, giving the CEO more time to manage the organization. The Chair can interact with external constituents, and can protect the CEO from individual board members who may become bullies. As Bowen said: "The CEO, after all, works for the board—and, therefore, for any bullies who may be on it. The chief executive should not have to deal personally with the inappropriate behavior of cantankerous board members."[85]

There are also legal requirements regarding for-profit corporations that prohibit the CEO from providing leadership in selecting new board members, evaluating the board and its members, supervising the work of the audit committee, and evaluating and compensating the CEO.

"Independent" or "outside" directors could do it, but it makes sense for it to be done by a Chair who is not the CEO.

Perhaps the best argument for separation of the roles is that the roles are truly *different*. Board judgments are valuable because they are not the judgments of inside administrators. To combine the roles is to lose the unique advantages of each.

The chair serves the board

If there is a double role for the chair, it is a double role within the board itself. John Carver, in his essay, *The Unique Double Servant Leadership Role of the Board Chairperson*, pointed out that the board is a "group servant-leader" and the chairperson is a servant-leader, so the chair has a double role—"servant leadership squared." Carver argued that the board is the boss, not the chair. The chair is there to help the board to do its work. Carver said:

> In the beginning was the board. There is no chair until the board
> empowers a chair, which means the chair works at the pleasure of
> the board and has whatever authority the board chooses to give.
> And the 'value added' assigned to this newly created servant is the
> job of leadership! 'Lead us to be what we've decided to be. Lead
> us to produce what we've decided to produce. Impose upon us
> the discipline we've committed ourselves to.' The authority of the
> chair, in other words, comes from the board. The visible, dynamic,
> sometimes insistent leader is first servant.[86]

Carver argued that the chair needs to have personal integrity, intelligence and conceptual flexibility, mindfulness of group process, a disposition to servanthood, and the ability to confront and lead. The chair's role is to serve as staff to the board. Carver said:

> This kind of chair is guardian of group integrity, not worker of his
> or her own agenda. This kind of chair nurtures the ability of his
> or her boss—the board—to truly be and stay the boss. This kind
> of chair is a reflector of board discipline, like the moon shining by
> a light no less spectacular because it is only reflected. This kind of

chair never forgets that the conductor doesn't make the music.[87]

Greenleaf argued that the position of chair is so important that a very large organization will need a full-time board chair. He also suggested the establishment of a Chairman's Institute, at which the art of chairmanship would be researched and taught. New chairs would receive initial training, and then return to the Institute from time to time to maintain or update skills.

The board role can change as the organization changes

The role of the board can vary with the growth and development of the organization. When a corporation is established, the board may be very active as a "working board," making lots of detailed decisions, not only about the ends but also the means, and pitching in to implement the decisions. In fact, board members may temporarily fill the roles of administration and staff, until such time as staff can be hired. Many non-profit organizations begin this way, with little money but a handful of committed board members. As money is raised and programs are launched, the board can hire staff to assume some or all of the administrative burdens. Once staff members are hired, the board can step back and make sure that it is leading, not administering.

After the early stages of development, there is one time that the board may become very involved again in detailed operations, and that is in an emergency. If the organization is about to fail financially, or is under investigation for illegal activities, the board—as the body with legal responsibility and the authority to manage the organization—will need to assess the situation in detail. That may mean supporting the work of the CEO and the administration, or it may mean adopting specific instructions for the administration, or it may mean relieving the CEO or other administrative leaders so that new leadership can be found. It should also mean assessing the board's own performance, to better understand how the board failed to detect the problems before they became a crisis. Once the crisis is past, the board can return to its normal role.

5.

The Board and the Administration

Greenleaf wrote that "administrators are responsible for all actions necessary to reach the goals set by trustees."[88] He was specific about the functions of corporate administrators. He wrote that the usual administrative functions include:

   a. *Planning*—both strategic and tactical—to accomplish goals;
   b. *Organizing* the total effort (except the executive office, which is designed by the trustees—with the advice, of course, of administrators);
   c. *Controlling*—assembling and analyzing data and directing operations; and
   d. *Supporting* the above by functional staffs in research and development, law, public relations, personnel, finance, marketing, production, and so on.[89]

These functions are consistent with the concept that boards make policy and administrations implement those policies.

However, while identifying the role of boards and functions of administrations, Greenleaf gave the highest priority to leadership. Because leadership is so critical to the success of the organization, Greenleaf believed that leadership should be provided by everyone—trustees, administrators, and staff. He wrote:

> Trustees lead the administrators. Administrators lead the trustees and the staff. Also, sometimes, leadership comes from unexpected places and from people who theretofore were not suspected of having it.

Trustees lead but they do not administer.

Administrators both administer and lead.

Staffs both administer (because everyone makes some decisions, however small, about what should be done) and sometimes lead (because the structure is open enough for anyone to lead who can effectively assert leadership). Their primary function, however, is to perform the tasks of the institution.[90]

Leadership is so important that if the chairman and top executives cannot provide it, others should step in. Greenleaf said:

Leadership—going out ahead to show the way—is available to everyone in the institution who has the competence, values, and temperament for it, from the chairman to the least skilled person. Leadership is a more critical requirement for the chairman and for the top executive officers. However, if their leadership should not be adequate, and if the institution is faltering for want of leadership, then it is important that whoever is able to assert leadership should do so from wherever he or she is. Trustees and administrators are empowered to lead, but if they fail to lead, or if they falter, then the system should be open enough so that they can be challenged (and guided) by anyone who can help to show a better way.[91]

Thus, while Greenleaf described the respective roles of boards and administrators, he placed higher priority on the need for leadership, wherever it might come from.

The distinction between policy-making and implementation is useful. The board adopts policies and encourages the administration to implement those policies within certain stated parameters. However, in practice, the boundaries between policy and implementation are not always clear. One reason is that "policy" is hard to define. What level of detail is appropriate for a policy, and what level is appropriate for an administrative instruction or procedure? Another reason that the boundaries are not always clear is that boards and administrators may find themselves alternating in their leadership roles as they develop policies. For example, strategic planning may begin with recommendations from the administration, which are then worked on by the board, which are then returned to the administration for comment, and then finally adopted by the board. The board makes the policy, but it does so through an interactive process with the administration.

Not all experts accept the distinction between policy-making by the board and implementation by the administration. In their article on "The New Work of the Nonprofit Board," Barbara Taylor, Richard Chait, and Thomas Holland define the "new work" of the board as work that focuses on what truly matters. In doing that new work, boards and executives are partners:

> In the world of the old work, the lines were clearly drawn: the board remained on the policy-setting side of the net, management on the implementation side, and so the game of governance was played. In the new work, the board and management are on the same side of the net as partners in both roles. The question is not, Is this an issue of policy or implementation? Rather, the question is, Is the issue at hand important or unimportant, central or peripheral? [92]

The authors asserted that in the old work:

1. Management defines problems, assesses options, and proposes solutions. Board listens, learns, approves, and monitors.
2. Board sets policy, which management implements. Respective territories are sharply defined; there is little or no border traffic. Domains are decided by organization chart.[93]

By comparison, in the new work:

1. Board and management discover issues that matter, mutually determine the agenda, and solve problems together.
2. Board and management both set policy and implement it. Lines are blurred, borders open. Domains are decided by nature of issue at hand.[94]

This emphasis on what matters, rather than the roles of the board and administration, may be especially relevant to the governance of non-profit organizations. As Drucker noted, non-profits are focused on their missions. "Effective nonprofits do not talk much about policy. They talk about work. They define what each organ [board or management] is expected to perform and what results each organ is expected to achieve."[95] Work is the focus because it is the work that fulfills the mission.

The Board and the CEO

After serving on many for-profit and non-profit boards over the years, Bowen concluded:

> The quality of the working relationship between the CEO/ president and the board is *the* most important factor determining organizational effectiveness in both sectors. Successful governance is difficult, if not impossible, to achieve without a mutually rewarding partnership between the board and the organization's chief executive.[96]

David H. Smith said simply, "no organization can survive long if the board and CEO are at loggerheads."[97] According to BoardSource:

> Exceptional boards recognize that they cannot govern well without the chief executive's collaboration and that the chief executive cannot lead the organization to its full potential without the board's unflagging support. Exceptional boards forge a partnership with the chief executive characterized by mutual trust, forthrightness, and a common commitment to mission.[98]

BoardSource stated that "providing personal and organizational support for executive leadership, periodically assessing the chief executive's performance, and acknowledging superb service through appropriate compensation are key board responsibilities."[99] Boards should ensure that the CEO receives frequent feedback, feels that she or he is being assessed fairly, is introduced by board members to key community leaders, receives invitations to important social events, is complimented for exceptional initiatives, and is encouraged to take time for renewal. The board should also make sure that the CEO is confident that the board chair will intervene whenever board members abuse their position, and that the board chair is sensitive to personal situations and respects the confidentiality of private conversations between the chair and the CEO.[100]

Max De Pree, in *Called to Serve*, stated that boards owe four things to the president or chief administrator: mandate, trust, space, and care. He wrote:

> Our mandate should always include a mission statement and a strategy, both of which derive clearly from who we intend to be… The next elements of the president's mandate are the statement of expectation and a definition of what will be measured in his performance institutionally, professionally, and personally…Trust is an enormous treasure for any organization. The board surely owes this to its president or conductor, just as he surely owes it to the entire organization…Like everyone else, the leader of an organization needs space…One of the ways a board gives space is by establishing a workable structure…Another way for the board to create space for a president is to play a 'review and reflect' role in the selection, nurture, assignment, and evaluation of key people…
>
> The fourth thing the board owes the president is care…the kind of care that arises from…devotional bonding…; the kind of care that recognizes the needs of a president's family for friendship, support, and love; the kind of care that makes both vacations and regular health checkups mandatory; the kind of care that goes the extra mile in compensation arrangements to include such things as budgeted spouse travel allowance and financial planning service; the kind of care that sees the president's need for continuing education and development—especially the opportunity to be mentored—as crucial to the organization's future; and finally, the kind of care that keeps the president alive, that doesn't permit him to 'work himself to death.'[101]

Board members should promise and demonstrate that the board is committed to the president's success.

The board should also invite the CEO to comment on the ways in which the board's actions impact the CEO's effectiveness. Are the respective roles clear? What does the board do that makes it easier for the CEO to be effective? What does the board do that makes it harder for the CEO? Are there areas in which the CEO would like the board to provide more leadership? Are there areas in which the CEO believes that the board is too involved in management? Constructive comments from the CEO can improve board performance and the board-CEO relationship.

The Chair and the CEO

Greenleaf stated that no board member should be a "super-administrator," engaged in supervising the staff.[102] Carver agrees. He recommends that the board establish a written policy that clearly states that *no* board member has any authority over the CEO.[103]

Carver noted that "governance works much better if the chair is responsible for ensuring that the board accomplish its own job, rather than for overseeing the performance of the CEO."[104] The chair is staff to the board, and "this highly visible staff position, no matter how important it is to the board, can have no legitimate authority over line personnel— including the CEO and his or her employees."[105] The chair does not supervise the CEO, because it is the full board that instructs the CEO. The CEO works for the entire board, not just one member—even if that one member is the chair. Carver argues that one of the qualifications of a board chair should be that she or he has the ability to leave the CEO alone.[106]

One of the problems that can occur when the chair supervises the CEO is role reversal. If the board chair supervises the CEO, then *two* people are both trying to administer the organization. That can be confusing to the staff, as well as demoralizing to the CEO. Also, the chair may not be a good person to do any supervising, because she or he may not have the daily, detailed operating experience or the technical expertise to lead the administration.

Furthermore, if the board chair is busy supervising the CEO, the chair may not be spending enough time serving the board, which can create a vacuum of leadership at the board level. Oddly enough, the CEO may be drawn into leading the board, on an informal basis, to fill the vacuum left by the chair. But the CEO is not likely to have the perspective needed to do a good job filling the board leadership role. The result can be a situation in which the staff is being led by a chair who doesn't have the appropriate experience, and the board is being led by a CEO who doesn't have the appropriate perspective.

The chair and CEO should see each other as partners with different roles. They should discuss, understand, and agree upon those roles. Each should ask the other: "What can I do to help you to be effective?" Mutual support can build trust, which can serve as the foundation for the exchange of information and ideas, as well as the coordination of policy development and implementation. The chair should not supervise the CEO, and the CEO should not dominate the board. Instead, the chair should be the servant-leader of the board, and the CEO should be the servant-leader of the staff.

Drucker stated that the board and the executive "have to work as one team of equals."[107] However, in a non-profit organization, the executive officers are the stronger players, so "it is their job to adjust both what they do and how they do it to the personalities and strengths of their chairpersons."[108] As chairs and their interests change, the executive should change his or her priorities to cover the areas the chairs do not address.

Do those served grow as persons?

In his classic essay, *The Servant as Leader*, Greenleaf set forth the test of a servant-leader: "Do those served grow as persons? Do they, *while being served*, become healthier, wiser, freer, more autonomous, more likely themselves to become servants?"[109] Boards have the opportunity to help administrators and staff members to grow as persons and as professionals.

For example, boards can help administrators to understand how well they are doing in fulfilling their roles. Greenleaf wrote:

> Few of us, regardless of how able, have the ability to perform

consistently at a high level of excellence, to set goals for our own performance, and to judge our own performance objectively. It is not reasonable to expect an internal operating team to do all of these things well, simultaneously.[110]

Administrators can benefit from the board's detached, reasoned advice, and the board's examination of the administration's ideas. Board members can also offer new ideas, new connections, and new resources not known or available to administrators. As Taylor, Chait, and Holland stated, "knowledgeable trustees can help inform the CEO's judgment. They can also perform a useful function for the CEO by focusing the organization's attention on issues that are unpopular within it or that fall outside the staff's capabilities."[111]

Richard Broholm and Douglas Wysockey-Johnson, in their book, *A Balcony Perspective: Clarifying the Trustee Role*, use an image shared by leadership expert Ronald Heifetz. The image is of a balcony overlooking a dance floor. Boards can see things from the balcony that administrators cannot see when they are on the dance floor. One way in which board members can share their insights is to function as mentors to the staff. For example, trustees can:

- ask provocative questions that encourage staff to reflect broadly and in depth about their recommendations and proposals
- empower staff to be and do the best they possibly can, celebrating their achievements and encouraging them to use failure as an opportunity for learning and growth
- avoid second guessing staff about how best to manage the organization on a daily basis, and use their balcony perspective to help staff step back and see issues in a larger context
- create a climate of hospitality for reflection that nurtures trust within the organization and between it and the community to be served
- provide a safe environment where staff and trustees can reflect together on the consequences of action before acting
- ensure organizational talents are being used.[112]

Broholm and Wysockey-Johnson put forth this hypothesis:

> Although a trustee board legally holds ultimate power over an
> organization, the most effective way in which its power is exercised
> is when trustees see themselves as mentors to the organization and
> its staff, exercising ultimate authority to control decisions only in
> extreme cases where to act indecisively would put the organization
> and its service to the community at risk.[113]

Carver urges board members to remember that when they mentor staff
members, they are not issuing instructions, they are offering advice.
Instructions can only come from the full board.

Greenleaf knew that in addition to appointing and mentoring the top
administrative officers, the board needs to make sure that leaders are being
developed within the organization. He said:

> Every large institution that is to be optimal in its performance must
> produce leadership out of its own ranks…It should import some
> leaders and other trained persons in order to check inbredness and
> to keep the organization stimulated, not because it did not produce
> enough of its own.[114]

Ram Charan emphasized the board's responsibility in this regard. In his
book, *Boards that Deliver*, he said:

> Few boards delve into the leadership gene pool below the
> seniormost level, despite its importance to a company's performance
> and longevity. That's a mistake. Organizational competence cannot
> be left to chance. Boards have a duty to ensure that management
> is developing a leadership gene pool that is relevant, capable, up-
> to-date, and diverse enough to allow the company to meet a wide
> range of challenges. A business that appears healthy today can
> take a nosedive if good leaders throughout the company become
> demotivated or leave, or if the entire gene pool has the same skills
> and mindset and cannot adapt to new conditions. Once left to
> decline, the leadership gene pool takes a long time to rebuild.[115]

Necessary ambiguities and tensions

Greenleaf was aware of many of the ambiguities and tensions that exist in organizations. He noted that institutions are not wholly rational, and as a result, the ambiguities and tensions can paralyze an administration. Boards may need to intervene to prevent institutional paralysis.

The first ambiguity that Greenleaf described was "*the operational necessity to be both dogmatic and open to change.*"[116] There are so many things to decide, and so many situations to face, that it is necessary to be dogmatic—to tell people what to do and how to do it. This minimizes confusion. On the other hand, it is also necessary to be open to new ideas, or the organization may not survive. Since administrators are very competent in the current pattern of operations, it is harder for them to launch new ideas and lead the change process. Board members, who are not part of the day-to-day operations, are in a better position to do that. So administrators should be mostly dogmatic but a little bit open to change, while board members should be a little bit dogmatic but mostly open to change. "The two roles, closely linked and working in harmony, should take care of both today and tomorrow."[117]

The second ambiguity that Greenleaf described is "*the disability that goes with competence.*"[118] People who are good at what they do may be unable or unwilling to examine their operating assumptions. Administrators need to stay focused on the tasks at hand, and in doing so, may limit their peripheral vision. Boards need to examine the operating assumptions and, seeing the broader perspective, may need to set new goals.

The third ambiguity arises from "the need for a healthy *tension between belief and criticism* as part of the dynamism that makes a high-performing institution."[119] Administrators need to be mostly *believing*, because they need to sustain morale and communicate the rightness of what is being done. On the other hand, board members need to be mostly *critical*, asking questions, testing assumptions, and challenging the status quo, to keep the institution on a true course. As Bowen says, one of the central tasks of either a for-profit or non-profit board is "a more or less constant questioning of basic assumptions and priorities."[120]

Greenleaf did not suggest there is any way to resolve these ambiguities. They are built into the roles of the board and the administration. Board members and administrators should learn to live with them, because organizations need to be both dogmatic and open to change; they need competence, even with its disabilities; and they need both belief and criticism.

It has been my experience that the ambiguity between the administration role of believing and the board role of being critical is frustrating but exceptionally important. The typical situation may be something like this. The board has decided that the organization needs to accomplish a certain task or create a certain program—let's call it Program X. The CEO therefore becomes focused on the task. She works with the administrative leadership team, holding meetings, identifying the issues, laying out the budget, designing the training, and helping everyone in the organization to understand X, why it is important, and how it can best be accomplished. There are problems—there are fires to put out and crises to resolve—but the administration and staff stay focused, morale is good, and the organization steadily implements X. There is a strong belief in the importance of X and the organization's ability to make it work.

Then at a board meeting a year or two later, the board asks: Is X really the right program? There are shifts in social, economic, environmental, and political trends. There are new needs and new opportunities to make a difference. And every program, product, or service has its own life cycle— introduction, growth, maturity, and decline. So do we still want to do X? How about Y or Z? And isn't X turning out to be more expensive than we thought—requiring more cash and human resources than we originally estimated? Is it as good a return on our resources as we should be getting? The board is critical.

The CEO may not be happy when board members ask these questions. After all, the board decided on X, the administration and staff have been working hard to implement X, and the organization is moving forward, in spite of some unforeseen circumstances. It is frustrating when all that effort is questioned. But the board needs to ask these questions, and administrators need to answer them. The result is bound to be good for the organization.

There are two likely outcomes, and both of them are beneficial: Either (1) the CEO will be able to explain to the board why X still makes sense, in which case the board will have learned something, and will continue to support X, or (2) the CEO will *not* be able to explain why X still makes sense, in which case the CEO will have learned something—she will have learned that the organization should no longer be implementing X.

Administrators and staff want to make the best possible use of the organization's time and resources. If there are better opportunities than X for the organization to be of service, then the CEO should want to know what those opportunities are, in order to learn about them and then work on them. The board can lead the administration by asking the big questions about the organization's purpose, problems, and opportunities. The questions will imply criticism, but that is the board's role. The administration's role is to work on the answers to the board's questions, and enter into a dialogue with the board to discuss whatever is learned.

When administrations do *not* respond to questions, it becomes frustrating for board members. They may see administrators as recalcitrant and even arrogant, not wanting to share information with the board, or unwilling to honestly examine their assumptions. Board members can tell when the administration believes that the board should not be asking questions—that the board should just quickly and politely rubber stamp whatever the administration proposes. Unfortunately, board members often accept the recalcitrance and even arrogance of administrators. The results can be sad, even tragic, for the organization.

Over the years I have served on several boards whose members did not ask questions. They did not probe dubious assumptions, even when they admitted privately that the administration's assumptions made no sense to them. When I asked questions and probed, it made the other board members uncomfortable. They knew that questions should be asked, but they didn't want to appear to be critical or embarrass the CEO. So the board didn't make the contribution that it could have made to the success of the organization. The board's time and talent was wasted. In each case, I politely resigned, or declined to be nominated for another term. Years later, I saw that the organizations were suffering—in several cases, very severely—

from failing to address the issues that all of us on the board knew were key issues.

While there are necessary ambiguities and tensions between boards and administrators, the relationship can be productive, exciting, and rewarding. The honest and open sharing of information and ideas between boards and administrators can build trust, and can be extremely stimulating and constructive. Ram Charan wrote:

> Boards add value through open, trusting dialogue—among directors and between directors and the management team (including the CEO, of course). The content of that dialogue must be significant to the success of the business. When the dialogue is focused on issues of strategy, organizational capability, and performance against objectives, when the best minds are allowed to absorb information, ask questions, and probe the assumptions, when every person in the room speaks with candor and listens with respect, the excitement builds and the energy flows. The intellectual output is superb.[121]

Once trust is established between board members and administrators, extraordinary dialogue is possible, and that dialogue almost always leads to new ideas and greater opportunities for the organization. As Bowen said:

> Boards of directors and trustees are…the steering devices for complex organizations—with the potential to guide them down right or wrong paths. Their job is by no means only to help organizations avoid serious missteps; they also need to be proactive partners in working with the CEO/president to achieve highly positive outcomes.[122]

Those positive outcomes are possible when boards and administrators work together to support the goals, plans, policies, and programs that are adopted. Since agreement is not always possible or always complete, that mutual support requires loyalty and discipline. *It also requires servant hearts*—the recognition that the goals, plans, policies, and programs are not about board members or administrators, but about the people the organization serves.

6.

The Effective Board

A Team at the Top

Greenleaf argued that the board will be most effective when it is a team, a council of equals. Greenleaf said that *"no man or woman is complete; no one of them is to be entrusted with all. Completeness is to be found only in the complemental talents of several who relate as equals."*[123]

Jon R. Katzenbach and Douglas K. Smith, in *The Wisdom of Teams: Creating the High-Performance Organization*, agreed with Greenleaf. They defined a team as "a small group of people (typically fewer than twenty) with complementary skills committed to a common purpose and set of specific performance goals."[124] They argued that teams should be the basic unit of performance for most organizations, because "teams outperform individuals acting alone or in large organizational groupings, especially when performance requires multiple skills, judgments, and experiences."[125] They noted that "most models of the 'organization of the future'…are premised on teams surpassing individuals as the primary performance unit in the company."[126]

Why do teams perform so well? Katzenbach and Smith provided four reasons:

> First, they bring together complementary skills and experiences that, by definition, exceed those of any individual on the team. This broader mix of skills and know-how enables teams to respond to multifaceted challenges like innovation, quality, and customer service. Second, in jointly developing clear goals and approaches,

teams establish communications that support real-time problem solving and initiative...Third, teams provide a unique social dimension that enhances the economic and administrative aspects of work. Real teams do not develop until the people in them work hard to overcome barriers that stand in the way of collective performance. By surmounting such obstacles together, people on teams build trust and confidence in each other's capabilities...Both the meaning of work and the effort brought to bear upon it deepen, until team performance eventually becomes its own reward. Finally, teams have more fun...What distinguishes the fun of teams is how it both sustains and is sustained by team performance...[127]

Teamwork at the board level is a key to effectiveness, and it is not easy to achieve. Greenleaf knew that "if trustees posit a role for themselves that will enable them to be influential in raising the performance of the total institution to the optimal...they confront a difficult problem: how to carry that role *as a group*."[128]

In their book, *Improving the Performance of Governing Boards*, Richard Chait, Barbara Taylor, and Thomas Holland stated that "the corporate concept of the *group* as the decision-making entity constitutes a core value and fundamental tenet of trusteeship."[129] BoardSource stated: "Governance is group action. Individual board members do not govern the organization. Rather, meeting as a group confers governing status to the board as a whole."[130]

John and Miriam Carver asserted that a key to operating successfully as a group is an understanding that "the board speaks with one voice or not at all."[131] If the board is going to make authoritative decisions, it must have a single voice. The Carvers said:

> This one-voice principle does not mean that there should be unanimity or lack of diversity on the board. On the contrary...the board must embrace all of the diversity it can and then reach out to obtain more. Differences among trustees are not only to be respected, but encouraged. Rarely will a vote be unanimous. Those trustees who lose a vote, however, must accept that the board has

spoken and that its decision must be implemented as decided.[132]

As John Carver said, "no one board member has any right at all over the organization governed."[133] Every voice is heard, but board members understand that they do not have individual power or authority. Even the chair should only speak for the board after the board has deliberated and voted. This is respectful of the fact that the powers granted by charters of incorporation are granted to the full board, and only the *full board* has decision-making authority.

The characteristics of effective boards

What are the specific characteristics of effective boards? Richard Chait, Thomas Holland, and Barbara Taylor set out to answer this question by studying the boards of colleges and universities, beginning in the late 1980s. In *The Effective Board of Trustees*, they reported on their results after three years of research with 108 board members and presidents. They found that there are specific characteristics and behaviors that distinguish strong boards from weak boards. The differences were classified into six distinct dimensions or competencies: contextual, educational, interpersonal, analytical, political, and strategic.

In the contextual dimension, "the board understands and takes into account the culture and norms of the organization."[134] The board relies on the institution's mission, values, and traditions as a guide in making decisions. In the educational dimension, "the board takes the necessary steps to ensure that trustees are well-informed about the institution, the profession, and the board's roles, responsibilities, and performance."[135] The board creates opportunities for trustee education, and seeks feedback on its own performance.

In the interpersonal dimension, "the board nurtures the development of trustees *as a group*, attends to the board's *collective* welfare, and fosters a sense of cohesiveness."[136] The board creates a sense of inclusiveness, develops group goals, and cultivates leadership. In the analytical dimension, "the board recognizes complexities and subtleties in the issues it faces and draws upon multiple perspectives to dissect complex problems and to synthesize appropriate responses."[137] The board approaches problems from a broad institutional outlook, searches widely for information, seeks different viewpoints, and recognizes that complex issues rarely offer perfect solutions.

In the political dimension, "the board accepts as one of its primary responsibilities the need to develop and maintain healthy relationships among key constituencies."[138] The board respects the legitimate roles of other stakeholders, communicates directly with key constituencies, and attempts to minimize win/lose situations. In the strategic dimension, "the board helps envision and shape institutional direction and helps ensure a strategic approach to the organization's future."[139] The board concentrates on processes that sharpen priorities, directs its attention to decisions of strategic magnitude, and acts before issues become urgent.

After identifying the characteristics of effective boards, Chait, Holland, and Taylor designed an action research study to answer the question: Can boards of trustees learn to improve, to become more competent? In their book, *Improving the Performance of Governing Boards*, they defined effective governance as "a collective effort, through smooth and suitable processes, to take actions that advance a shared purpose consistent with the institution's mission."[140] Effective boards make decisions and take actions "that enhance the long-term quality, vitality, and stability of the institution...the best boards add the most value..."[141]

According to Chait, Holland, and Taylor, the best boards add value through five interrelated approaches: (1) they help senior management determine what matters most; (2) they create opportunities for the president to think aloud; (3) they encourage experimentation; (4) they monitor progress and performance; and (5) they model the desired behaviors.[142]

The authors concluded that boards can improve their performance, but board development cannot be imposed on either the trustees or the institution's president. Board development has to be embedded in important issues and substantive agendas. While a board's attitude or a trustee's personality may be hard to change, a board can change its *behaviors*. New structures, information systems, channels of communication, and orientation programs can help trustees to act and think differently. Above all, board development must be an intensive, long-term process.

Focusing on what matters

In their article in the *Harvard Business Review* on "The New Work of the Nonprofit Board," Taylor, Chait, and Holland stated that "a board's contribution is meant to be strategic, the joint product of talented people brought together to apply their knowledge and experience to the major challenges facing the institution."[143] The key to improved performance is therefore to focus on work that really matters. This "new work" has four characteristics:

> First, it concerns itself with crucial, do-or-die issues central to the institution's success. Second, it is driven by results that are linked to defined timetables. Third, it has clear measures of success. Finally, it requires the engagement of the organization's internal and external constituencies.[144]

The authors argued that it is not enough to scrutinize management. The board must find out what really matters. Board members and management need to determine the important issues. They need to review the organization's foremost strategic challenges, get to know key stakeholders, and consult experts about the economics, demographics, and politics of the industry in which the organization operates. Having identified what matters, the board and management should establish ten to twelve critical indicators of success, and then monitor them.

The board should organize itself around the institution's priorities. Committees, work groups, and task forces must address strategic priorities. Board meetings should be goal-driven, and focus on what matters most. And board members should be chosen with an eye to the overall chemistry of the board. A board should not consist of individual stars, nor should it be run by a powerful inner circle. A board should be a constellation of members who are involved and contributing to the total team effort. As Max De Pree said, "structure is important, but what is much more important—in fact, critical—is the willingness and ability of the people involved to establish and maintain amiable and productive relationships."[145]

One of the benefits of focusing on what matters is that board members will be more engaged and committed. Board members want to make a difference. When it is clear that their work is having significant impacts, they find the work more meaningful and enjoyable. Max De Pree observed that "when an organization demands true leadership and the results justify the time and energy, good boards respond with gusto."[146]

In the Policy Governance® Model, the board focuses on what matters by debating and identifying its most important values, which are then organized into four categories of policies: ends, executive limitations, board-staff linkage, and governance process. By systematically establishing these policies, the board identifies what it considers to be of most importance. These policies create a proactive framework for the staff, which can then develop and adjust its plans as necessary, so long as they are consistent with the board's policies. The result is that the board does not find itself being drawn into administrative details, approving and then re-approving the staff's plans. The board merely needs to make sure that the staff's plans are in compliance with the board's ends and executive limitations. The rest of the time, the board can focus on the policies that it has established to reflect its most important values.[147]

What do board members need to know to be effective?

Focusing on what matters is not easy when board members do not have in-depth knowledge of the issues that the organization faces. C. Northcote Parkinson, in his satire *Parkinson's Law*, identified the Law of Triviality, by which "the time spent on any item of the agenda will be in inverse proportion to the sum involved." This occurs because people don't understand the big, expensive items on the agenda, so they focus their time on the smaller, inexpensive items that they do understand. Parkinson described a finance committee that devoted a lot of time to arguing about the construction of a bicycle shed for the use of the clerical staff, which was estimated to cost $2,350. However, the committee devoted only two and a half minutes to a discussion of the construction of an atomic reactor, which cost $10,000,000. The challenge, of course, is to provide enough information to board members so that they will understand the big items, and will give those items more attention than the trivial ones.[148]

Robert Greenleaf was concerned about the information that board members receive. He said:

> …Nominal trustees customarily accept, somewhat uncritically, data supplied by internal officers and take no steps to equip themselves to be critical. They restrict themselves to affirming goals that are set by administrators and staffs, and, with the exception of the certified audit, trustees largely confine themselves to reviewing performance through administrators' reports on their own work, with little independent data available to them except what they sense intuitively or gather from the 'grapevine.' When there are adverse conditions, sometimes trustees are the last to know—and they should be among the first. Consequently they may rest comfortably with the illusion that the administration of the institution is functioning much better than may actually be the case.[149]

Ram Charan agrees. In *Boards that Deliver*, he wrote:

> Directors are uniformly frustrated by the low quality of information they get. Sometimes they get a hundred-page packet filled with jargon and financial minutiae a week before a meeting. Sometimes they have difficulty getting any information at all from management.
>
> Whether the data is too much, too little, or too poorly presented, boards spend a lot of board meeting time questioning management about the meaning of data they have received…This leaves directors unprepared for substantive discussion, even if there were plenty of time for it.[150]

By contrast, as BoardSource pointed out, "exceptional boards institutionalize a culture of inquiry, mutual respect, and constructive debate that leads to sound and shared decision making…Exceptional boards seek more information, question assumptions, and challenge conclusions so that they may advocate for solutions based on analysis."[151]

Boards need to work with administrators to determine in advance what information board members need. When board members understand the meaning and the context of the information before the meeting, the board meeting can be used to "discuss the future of the company as the information indicates, rather than discussing the meaning of the information itself."[152]

Charan recommended five channels of information for boards: (1) a succinct report or board briefing before the meeting; (2) a short letter from the management on current conditions, (3) periodic surveys of employees; (4) visits by directors to company stores or plants to talk directly with line managers and experience the business firsthand; and (5) reports from board committees with recommendations and background information.[153]

Board members need to know whatever is relevant to their functions— setting goals and defining obligations, appointing the top executive officers and designing the top administration, assessing the total performance of the organization, and then acting on what is learned during their assessment. They will, of course, want the information and recommendations provided by administrators and staff members, but board members will also want information from other sources, so they can make independent judgments, including judgments contrary to what the administration is recommending.

Board members need to be active listeners. Robert Greenleaf said that "only a true natural servant automatically responds to any problem by listening *first*."[154] By asking and then listening, servant-leaders are able to identify the needs of their colleagues and those the organization serves. Servant-leaders in the boardroom can make an important contribution to the organization by asking and seeking answers to questions like these:

Colleagues/Employees
- How well are we serving our employees? How do we know?
- Do they have the resources they need to provide quality service to others?
- How often and in what ways do we listen to our employees?
- How well do we respond to what we hear from our employees?
- How do we help our employees grow as persons?
- How can we do better?

Customers/Clients/Members/Patients/Students/Citizens
- Who is our organization serving? Why?
- How well are we serving them? How do we know?
- Do we have the resources we need to provide them with high quality programs, products, and services?
- How often and in what ways do we listen to those we serve?
- How well do we respond to what we hear from those we serve?
- How do we help those we serve to grow as persons?
- How can we do better?
- Are there others we should also be serving? Why? If so, what do they need? How do we know?
- If there are others we should be serving, what resources will be required to serve them? How can we get those resources?

Business Partners/Shareholders/Communities
- What impact is our organization having on our business partners, shareholders, and the communities in which we operate? How do we know?
- How can we have a more positive impact?
- What programs and resources do we need to have a more positive impact?

Servant-leaders in the boardroom keep their organizations closely connected with everyone the organization touches. Understanding the needs of each group is essential to effectiveness, efficiency, and the long-term success of the organization. To understand the needs of each group, the board should gather information from all stakeholders, especially those the organization serves directly. That may mean interviewing stakeholders, visiting sites at which the organization operates, and meeting employees, customers, shareholders or members, business partners, and community members. As Max DePree pointed out: "There is no better way for a board member to learn what is going on in a corporation or a non-profit group than to spend a couple of days with a customer."[155]

In gathering this information, boards should not appear to be investigating or seeking to evaluate the performance of the senior leadership of their organizations. The board and CEO can work together to design the information-gathering process, and jointly announce to the members of the organization and its constituents that the process is going to take place. The emphasis should be on the board's desire to understand the organization and the people it serves, so that it can lead effectively. If similar information-gathering processes are used on a regular basis, it will not appear to be an effort to critique the administration. It may be best if the CEO and other senior administrative leaders are not present during each meeting with staff or constituents, to promote candor. However, the findings of the board's information-gathering process should be shared with the CEO and senior leaders.

One of the key practices of servant-leaders is foresight. Greenleaf said that "prescience, or foresight, is a better than average guess about *what* is going to happen *when* in the future."[156] He said that foresight is the "lead" that the leader has. Without foresight, a leader is not leading—he or she is only reacting. And a leader who is only reacting to events may run out of options, and get boxed in, and start making bad decisions, including unethical ones. That is why Greenleaf said that foresight is the central ethic of leadership. A failure of foresight can put an organization in a bad situation that might have been avoided.

Exercising foresight may require consultation with experts outside the organization who can brief the board on trends in demographics, government regulations, the economy, the political environment, and other issues that affect the work of the organization. However the information is obtained, it is essential that boards study underlying trends that can affect their organizations in the future.

Greenleaf believed that the board of a large organization should have its own permanent, independent staff as well as consultants who can help the board collect and analyze the information it needs. He wrote:

> Since there is no dependable information source responsible directly to them, most trustee bodies have no adequate way of examining performance. Furthermore, if trustees should decide to set goals, rather than simply to affirm or reject those brought to them by internal officers, they usually do not have the staff help they would

require to perform that service.[157]

The staff, as well as independent research firms and consultants, should be hired by the board and report directly to board members.

Greenleaf was so concerned about the effectiveness of boards that he suggested continuous coaching. He said:

> …a trustee board will do well to search for a *coach* who will help them learn an appropriate process so that they will become an effective collegial group whose judgment deserves to be respected as superior wisdom in matters which trustees should consider and decide. Since no group will ever achieve this fully, the coaching process will be continuous…

> The primary aim of the coach is to facilitate consensus—achieving one mind. The effective trustee group is not merely one that hears all of the arguments and then votes. Rather, it reaches a consensus—a group judgment that will be accepted as superior wisdom. Without the acceptance of all constituencies that trustee judgment is superior wisdom there is little leadership possible for trustees. Part of the acceptance of trustee judgment as superior wisdom rests upon a consistent group process that is carefully monitored by a coach.

> There is very little sustained performance at the level of excellence—of any kind, anywhere—without continuous coaching. Since trustees have the obligation to monitor the performance of the institution, and since trustees are the court of last resort, trustees who want to do the best they can will provide for the monitoring of their own work. *And this is how they will learn.*[158]

Problems and pitfalls

Creating and maintaining an effective board is a significant challenge. Chait, Holland, and Taylor stated:

After 10 years of research and dozens of engagements as consultants to nonprofit boards, we have reached a rather stark conclusion: *effective governance by a board of trustees is a relatively rare and unnatural act.* We mean no disrespect by this statement. Most trustees are bright and earnest individuals. However, the tides of trusteeship carry boards in the wrong direction: from strategy toward operations, from long-term challenges toward immediate concerns, from collective action toward individual initiatives…Regrettably, most boards just drift with the tides. As a result, trustees are often little more than high-powered, well-intentioned people engaged in low-level activities. The board dispatches an agenda of potpourri tied tangentially at best to the organization's strategic priorities and central challenges.[159]

The authors reported that board members themselves complained that most of the issues they dealt with were trivial, board meetings were boring, and they had plenty of information but didn't know what it meant. Furthermore, board members didn't act like players on the same team. Instead, "each committee or clique engages in a self-contained event on a common terrain, largely oblivious to the activities of others."[160]

Anyone who has served on a board, worked for a board, or done business with a board, is aware of the pitfalls and problems that can arise. De Pree described board members by saying: "Good people disagree, do a little politicking, try to make decisions in the bathroom (the worst form of exclusion), and come to meetings totally unprepared."[161]

I have served on several dozen boards in the public, private, and non-profit sectors. Most of the board members I have worked with have been genuinely interested in advancing the organization. However, over the years I have seen:

- Cliques of board members who fought each other during and outside board meetings, making it very hard for the board to get any work done.
- Board members who sought their positions on the board in order to "grandstand" before the press and gain public visibility that would

help them launch their political careers.
- Board members who brought their personal philosophical or ideological agendas to board meetings, and tried to cut off any opposing views.
- Board members who wanted to be "in with the in crowd" and therefore did not speak up when they opposed an issue favored by "the in crowd."
- Board members who used their board positions to generate business for their private companies.
- A board member who tried to pressure the executive officer of the institution into publicly supporting the board member's personal business project, which was totally unrelated to the institution.
- A board member who came to board meetings to get information that he could use in launching his own competing organization.

Board members are human beings, and some succumb to a variety of temptations relating to personal gain. A few even seem to think that the whole point of being on a board is to seize the personal benefits. When boards have members who are focused on their personal agendas or advantages, board meetings easily become contentious, petty, and ineffective.

Building a board of servant-leaders

The solution to the problems and pitfalls is to recruit board members who are servant-leaders—people who know that board meetings are not about board members, but are about advancing the institution and making a difference in the lives of others. To be effective in fulfilling the public trust, boards should seek out, and then select or elect, servant-leaders who have a passion for the organization and those it serves. Specifically, boards should:

1. Seek individuals who share a belief in the mission and values of the organization, but can bring different perspectives to the development of goals and the evaluation of the organization's performance. Build a board whose members have different backgrounds and fields of expertise. Build a board that is diverse in ethnicity, gender, and age. Find board members who are respectful, but are willing to speak the truth as they see it, even

if the truths they speak are awkward for others to hear. Find board members who work well with others, but are sufficiently independent-minded that they "do not allow their votes to be unduly influenced by loyalty to the chief executive or by seniority, position, or reputation of fellow board members, staff, or donors."[162]

2. Cultivate prospective board members by drawing them into the work of the organization and the board before they are invited to become board members. Invite them to lunch to get to know them, and solicit their advice. Ask them to serve as non-board members on committees. Learn about their experience on other boards. Find out how they are viewed by their peers. Discover if they really want to *serve*.

3. Seek board members who are willing to offer their time, talent, and treasure *as team members*. A group of stars, no matter how valuable individually, may not add up to a good team. Taylor, Chait, and Holland pointed out that "prospective trustees should understand that governance is a collective enterprise."[163] Look for a good fit. For example, prospective board members who run their own organizations, and are used to making their own decisions, may not be happy being part of a team with a group decision-making processes. Bowen warned that "not all capable people are good board members."[164]

Instead of recruiting busy board members by saying that little will be expected of them, boards should make it clear that a major commitment is being sought. Prospective board members are being asked to hold the charter of public trust for the organization, a responsibility that is to be taken seriously.

To remain strong, boards should conduct self-assessments, and identify steps that can be taken to improve. Boards should be willing to ask individual board members to leave if they are disruptive or have not been able to attend meetings or contribute in other ways. To continually renew the board's perspectives, the board should consider term limits on board service, so that new board members can join without increasing the board's size.

Boards should make sure the passion and purpose are maintained. Specifically, boards should:

1. Continually focus on the institution's mission and values.
2. Include time during board meetings to talk about the ways in which the organization serves the public good through its programs, products, and services.
2. Provide data and anecdotes that demonstrate the ways in which the board and the organization are making a difference in the lives of others.
4. Gently remind board members that board service is a high calling that demands commitment, integrity, and vision.

After gathering information, analyzing it, and discussing it, Boards must be committed to act. As Greenleaf wrote:

> Who is the enemy?...Who is responsible for the mediocre performance of so many of our institutions?..Not evil people. Not stupid people. Not apathetic people. Not the 'system...'
>
> The real enemy is fuzzy thinking on the part of good, intelligent, vital people, and their failure to lead, and to follow servants as leaders. Too many settle for being critics and experts. There is too much intellectual wheel spinning, too much retreating into 'research,' too little preparation for and willingness to undertake the hard and high risk tasks of building better institutions in an imperfect world, too little disposition to see 'the problem' as residing *in here* and not *out there.*
>
> *In short, the enemy is strong natural servants who have the potential to lead but do not lead, or who choose to follow a non-servant.* They suffer. Society suffers. And so it may be in the future. [65]

The unifying dream

Finally, boards should create a dream that is worthy of the board, the organization, and those it serves. That dream, based on the mission, should be a vision that unites the board. Compared to the dream, pettiness will appear to be what it is—petty.

In his essay, *The Leadership Crisis*, Greenleaf said:

> ...Institutions function better when the idea, the dream, is to the fore, and the person, the leader, is seen as the servant of the idea. It is not 'I,' the ultimate leader, that is moving this institution to greatness; it is the dream, the great idea. 'I' am subordinate to the idea; 'I' am servant of the idea along with everyone else who is involved in the effort... The leader leads well when leadership is, and is seen as, serving the dream and searching for a better one... It is the *idea* that unites people in the common effort, not the charisma of the leader. It is the communicated faith of the leader in the dream that enlists dedicated support needed to move people toward accomplishment of the dream...

> If the dream has the quality of greatness, it not only provides the overarching vision for the undertaking; it also penetrates deeply into the psyches of all who are drawn to it and savor its beauty, its rightness, and its wisdom. The test of greatness in a dream is that it has the energy to lift people out of their moribund ways to a level of being and relating from which the future can be faced with more hope than most of us can summon today.[166]

With the dream clearly in focus, it is easier for board members to see that it is not about *them*. It is about fulfilling the public trust, and making life better for *others*.

7.

The Call to Serve

If you are a servant-leader looking for an opportunity to make the world a better place, consider serving on a board. If you are already a board member, the opportunity to be a servant-leader is right in front of you.

Service on a board is an opportunity to lead a servant-institution and fulfill the public trust. It is an opportunity to learn and grow while doing meaningful work that has a significant impact on others.

To be an effective servant-leader in the boardroom, you must understand the purpose of the organization and support its mission and values. You must understand the role of the board, the role of the administration, and the ways in which the board and administration can be most effective. You must spend time preparing for meetings, participating in meetings, monitoring financial performance, working on strategic issues, testing ideas, building relationships for the organization, and setting high standards of excellence and service. You must really listen to the people your organization touches, and you must exercise foresight, so that your organization will continue to serve them well, long into the future.

Being a servant-leader in the boardroom requires a significant commitment. Greenleaf knew that it was essential that board members really care about their institutions. He said:

> Some power is essential. And to do what only a trustee can do you have to get to be a trustee. But most important of all is *caring*. Most trustees I know just don't care enough. If trustees really cared, ideas and people would blossom all over the place. *I know*. I have worked

inside institutions, several of them, where trustees did not care…
Also, I know because I have been a trustee in several situations
where *I* did not care—not enough. And I am keenly aware of
what unrewarding experiences those were—for *me* as an ineffective
trustee.[167]

Greenleaf saw the importance of boards, and hoped that committed
servant-leaders would decide to become board members as their avenue of
service. Board membership is more than an honor, or an opportunity to rub
shoulders with some interesting people, or in some cases an opportunity to
earn extra income. It is an opportunity to hold the charter of public trust for
the organization, to care about the institution, and to make sure that it does
well by everyone it touches—its employees, customers, business partners,
shareholders or members, and communities.

Board service is not for everyone. But it may be the right avenue of
service for you. If you are not already a board member, ask yourself: Is
board service my opportunity to serve, to make the world a better place?

If you are already a board member, what motivates you? What dreams
do you have? How can you help your organization to be a better servant-
institution? What legacy do you want to leave? What do you need to do to
make that contribution or leave that legacy? What is the next step you plan
to take?

Make a commitment to take that next step *now*.

This page intentionally left blank

Appendix

KEY REMINDERS FOR SERVANT-LEADERS IN THE BOARDROOM

1. Your corporation exists to serve others—staff or employees inside the corporation, and customers, clients, patients, members, students, or citizens outside the corporation.
2. Your corporation, whether for-profit or not-for-profit, was created by the government for the public good.
3. You and the other members of your board hold the charter of public trust for your corporation.
4. You and the other members of your board hold the legal authority to manage your corporation.
5. To be a servant-leader in the boardroom, you must be strongly committed to the mission and values of your organization, and care deeply about the ways in which your organization serves all the people it touches. You must be willing to devote a significant amount of time to board service.
6. Your board should truly lead, not simply approve staff recommendations.
7. Your board's judgments should add their own unique value to the corporation.
8. To be effective, your board must give priority to issues that truly matter.
9. Your board should govern on three levels: fiduciary, strategic, and generative.
10. Your board should be a council of equals, a team that invites and draws out the best in each board member. Your chair should serve

the board as "first among equals."

11. No individual board member has authority. Only the full board has authority.

12. Your board should determine the policies, and the administration should implement the policies.

13. You and the other members of your board should be mostly open to change, while the administration should be mostly dogmatic; you should be mostly critical, while the administration should be mostly believing.

14. The quality of the relationship between the board and the CEO is an important factor in your corporation's success.

15. No individual board member supervises the CEO. Only the full board instructs the CEO.

16. The chair should not supervise the CEO, and the CEO should not dominate the board. The chair and CEO should be partners. The chair should be servant-leader to the board, and the CEO should be servant-leader to the staff.

17. You and your fellow board members should ask questions, listen, and learn all that you can about the needs of your corporation's employees and the customers, clients, patients, members, students, or citizens that you all serve.

18. You should build your board by seeking out and cultivating servant-leaders who are diverse in ethnicity, gender, age, background, skill, insight, and expertise. Invite into board membership those who are respectful, but willing to speak the truth as they see it.

19. You should create a dream that is consistent with the corporation's mission and inspires and unifies the board.

20. Every day, you should remember that no matter how difficult it may become, you and the other members of your board can find meaning and satisfaction in making a difference in the lives of your corporation's staff and the people that you have joined together to serve.

THE SHAREHOLDER PRIMACY ISSUE

Greenleaf believed that board members should consider the interests of all stakeholders. He said that board members should be concerned with everyone that an organization touches—employees, customers, business partners, shareholders or members, and communities. Board members "are accountable to all parties at interest for the best possible performance of the institution in the service of the needs of all constituencies—including society at large. They are holders of the charter of public trust for the institution."[168]

However, many disagree. They argue that in for-profit corporations, shareholders deserve primary consideration over all other stakeholders. According to Lynn A. Stout, Paul Hastings Professor of Corporate and Securities Law at the University of California at Los Angeles School of Law:

> Of all the controversies in U.S. corporate law, one has proven most fundamental and enduring. This is, of course, the debate over the proper purpose of the public corporation. Should the public company seek only to maximize the wealth of its shareholders (the so-called 'shareholder primacy' view)? Or should public corporations be run in a manner that considers the interests of other corporate 'stakeholders' as well, including employees, consumers, even the larger society?[169]

A review of the law and related research suggests that shareholder primacy is not the position taken by most state legislatures and courts, and it is a position that can result in unethical behavior. The better view is "board primacy" or "director primacy."

Dodge v. Ford Motor Company

D. Gordon Smith, Associate Professor of Law at Northwestern School of Law of Lewis & Clark College, described the shareholder primacy norm as follows: "Corporate directors have a fiduciary duty to make decisions that are in the best interests of the shareholders."[170] The case most often quoted by scholars in this regard is a 1919 case, *Dodge v. Ford Motor Company*, in which the Michigan Supreme Court upheld a lower court decision requiring the Ford Motor Company to pay additional dividends to shareholders. In its discussion of the case, the court said:

> A business corporation is organized and carried on primarily for the profit of the stockholders. The powers of the directors are to be employed for that end. The discretion of directors is to be exercised in the choice of means to attain that end, and does not extend to a change in the end itself, to the reduction of profits, or to the nondistribution of profits among stockholders in order to devote them to other purposes.[171]

This is the statement that is often quoted to support shareholder primacy. However, this statement did not determine the court's decision.

The lawsuit was brought by the Dodge brothers, who were shareholders in the Ford Motor Company. They began as suppliers to Ford, and then became competitors of Ford when they began producing their first Dodge Brothers cars in 1914.

The board of directors of Ford Motor Company was dominated by Henry Ford, who was the largest shareholder, with 58% of the shares. Henry Ford was willing to pay dividends to shareholders. In fact, he was paying regular dividends of 5% per month—60% per year—on the original invested capital stock of $2 million. He also paid a total of $41 million in special dividends between 1911 and 1915. Shareholders had received a return far, far greater than their original investments.

Henry Ford continued paying regular dividends, but decided to stop paying special dividends, in order to achieve his business goals. The public press in Detroit quoted him as saying:

> My ambition…is to employ still more men; to spread the benefits of this industrial system to the greatest possible number, to help them build up their lives and their homes. To do this, we are putting the greatest share of our profits back into the business.[172]

In addition to expanding the company's production facilities and hiring more employees, Henry Ford wanted to continue to raise the wages of company employees, and sell cars at lower and lower prices, so more people could afford to buy them.

The company had grown rapidly since its founding in 1903, and the profits were piling up. During 1916, the company earned a profit of $60 million, and had $52 million cash on hand. The Dodge brothers sued to force the distribution of the profit to shareholders. They wanted an injunction to prevent the Ford Motor Company from investing in expansion; a decree requiring that at least 75 percent of the profit be distributed to shareholders; and a decree that in the future, the company be required to distribute *all* of the earnings to shareholders, except small amounts needed for emergency purposes. In short, the Dodge Brothers not only wanted money, they wanted to stop Ford's growth as a competitor.

The court made it clear that it would not normally interfere with the decisions of a board regarding dividends, and it is not a violation of the law to allow profits to accumulate and be reinvested in the business. The court also said that it did not want to interfere with the business expansion that was being planned by the Ford Motor Company. However, the Ford board had gone too far in this case, by accumulating so much cash and sharing so little of it with the stockholders. The court affirmed the lower court ruling that $19 million must be paid out as dividends.

The interesting point to note is that the court awarded *less than 40%* of the surplus to the shareholders, while allowing Ford to keep most of the money—more than $30 million. That $30 million was available to the company to raise wages, expand the business, and lower prices. In short, the court gave the plaintiff shareholders only part of what they wanted.

Today, it is accepted law that:

> ...The mere fact that a corporation has a large surplus will not justify interference by the court, at the instance of a minority stockholder, to compel declaration of a dividend. A corporation has the right to choose to retain its surplus earnings to insure its financial stability

and for the effectuation of internal policies and programs if it does so in good faith… While the action of the directors may be reviewed by the courts upon a proper showing, it will be set aside only in case of bad faith or when arbitrary, oppressive, manifestly erroneous, or such as clearly to constitute an abuse of their discretion, an overstepping of their powers, or a disregard of their official duty. Relief is refused where such grounds do not clearly appear, irrespective of adverse effects of the corporate policy on complaining stockholders.[173]

Smith pointed out that what is significant about the "shareholder primacy" statement found in the *Dodge v. Ford Motor Company* court opinion is that it applied to a dispute between minority and majority shareholders in a closely-held corporation:

…The shareholder primacy norm was first used by courts to resolve disputes among majority and minority shareholders in closely held corporations. Over time this use of the shareholder primacy norm has evolved into the modern doctrine of minority oppression. This application of the shareholder primacy norm seems incongruous today because minority oppression cases involve conflicts among shareholders, not conflicts between shareholders and nonshareholders. Nevertheless, when early courts employed rules requiring directors to act in the interests of *all* shareholders—not just the majority shareholders—they were creating the shareholder primacy norm.[174]

The idea was, simply, that majority shareholders should not oppress minority shareholders in closely-held corporations. The idea was not that shareholders have primacy over all other stakeholders.

Since conflicts between majority and minority shareholders in publicly traded companies are far less common than in closely-held corporations, "the shareholder primacy norm is nearly irrelevant to the ordinary business decisions of modern corporations."[175] One reason is the business judgment rule. Under the business judgment rule, a board of directors acting in good faith, with reasonable care, is not liable for making mistakes of judgment.

The board is therefore not likely to be held liable for a decision that favors stakeholders who are not shareholders. According to Smith, "the universal application of the business judgment rule makes the shareholder primacy norm virtually unenforceable against public corporations' managers...It is nearly an iron-clad shield for directors of public corporations."[176]

Shareholders are not owners of the corporation

Shareholder primacy has been promoted by economists during the past forty years. The "Chicago School" of economists argued that the proper goal of corporate governance was "to make shareholders as wealthy as possible."[177] In 1970, Milton Friedman published an article in *The New York Times Magazine* entitled, "The Social Responsibility of Business Is to Increase its Profits."[178] In that article, he argued that corporate executives were responsible to the owners of the business "to make as much money as possible while conforming to the basic rules of society."[179] He assumed that the shareholders of the corporation were the owners of the business. Professor Stout disagreed, saying:

> Milton Friedman is a Nobel Prize-winning economist, but he obviously is not a lawyer. A lawyer would know that the shareholders do not, in fact, own the corporation. Rather, they own a type of corporate security commonly called 'stock.' As owners of stock, shareholders' rights are quite limited. For example, stockholders do not have the right to exercise control over the corporation's assets. The corporation's board of directors holds that right. Similarly, shareholders do not have any right to help themselves to the firm's earnings; the only time they can receive any payment directly from the corporation's coffers is when they receive a dividend, which occurs only when the directors decide to declare one. As a legal matter, shareholders accordingly enjoy neither direct control over the firm's assets nor direct access to them. Any influence they may have on the firm is indirect, through their influence on the board of directors...It is misleading to use the language of ownership to describe the relationship between a public firm and its shareholders.[180]

Professor Stout also rejected the argument that shareholders are the sole residual claimants of a corporation, entitled to payment after the firm has paid its employees, managers, and creditors to fulfill its contractual commitments to them. In fact, shareholders are only allowed to receive payments when the corporation has enough retained earnings or profits, and the board of directors decides to declare a dividend. In short, "shareholders of a public corporation are entitled to receive nothing from the firm *unless and until the board of directors decides that they should receive it.*"[181]

Shareholders have the right to vote, the right to sue, and the right to sell their shares. However, in regard to their voting rights:

> As a matter of law these are severely limited in scope, principally to the right to elect and remove directors. Shareholders have no right to select the company's CEO; they cannot require the company to pay them a single penny in dividends; they cannot vote to change or preserve the company's line of business; they cannot stop directors from squandering revenues on employee raises, charitable contributions, or executive jets; and they cannot vote to sell the company's assets or the company itself (although they may in limited circumstances vote to veto a sale or merger proposed by the board).[182]

If corporate officers and directors fail to maximize shareholder wealth, shareholders can sue. However:

> …Courts consistently permit directors to use corporate funds for charitable purposes; to reject business strategies that would increase profits at the expense of the local community; to avoid risky undertakings that would benefit shareholders at creditors' expense; and to fend off a hostile takeover at a premium price in order to protect employees or the community. Contrary to the shareholder primacy thesis, shareholders cannot recover against directors or officers for breach of fiduciary duty simply because those directors and officers favor stakeholders' interests over the shareholders' own.[183]

Problems with shareholder primacy

One problem with shareholder primacy is fairness. Most shareholders today have contributed literally nothing to the firms whose shares they hold. Let's say that Ms. Jones bought shares of stock when the company was starting up or was issuing new shares to finance expansion. By buying those shares, Ms. Jones indeed contributed to the success of the firm—she invested money that helped the firm to grow. But then Ms. Jones sold her shares to Mr. Smith, who later sold his shares to Ms. Kim, who then sold her shares—and on and on. Most shareholders buy as speculators or investors, hoping to make money or improve their financial assets. Of course they want the company to produce strong financial results, so that the price of company shares will remain high. But these speculators and investors have *not contributed to the company*. They have not created value. They simply hope to make money off the company's performance.

Meanwhile, employees come to work at the company every day, producing the programs, products, and services that the company sells. They are giving their daily lives to the firm. They are creating value. Without them, there would be nothing for the company to sell. Then there are the customers who keep buying the programs, products, or services. Without them, the business would go out of business, and shares would have no value at all. Then there are the business partners who reliably supply materials and services so that the company and its employees can perform well. The business could not succeed without them. And then there are the local communities where the company has offices or production facilities. The company takes advantage of local infrastructure and services provided by local governments. Some companies create adverse impacts on their local communities that cost those communities far more than the taxes that the companies pay.

Employees, customers, business partners, and communities are all *stakeholders*. They all have a stake in the success or failure of the corporation. And without their contributions, corporations cannot succeed. "Promoters" who start corporations realize this. In drafting corporate charters, they almost never include statements giving primacy to shareholders. Shareholders have no problem with that—they are still happy to invest in the new corporation. Professor Stout suspects that the reason is that "if the firm did mandate shareholder primacy in its charter, it would find it far more difficult to attract qualified, motivated, and loyal employees, managers, and even creditors."[184] Shareholders want the corporation to succeed, and they know that other stakeholders are crucial to success.

Stakeholders such as creditors, employees, managers, and local governments may receive direct compensation, but they also have expectations about the future that are not reduced to writing. It is in the shareholders' interests to encourage these non-shareholders to continue their contributions after the corporation is up and running. Over the long term, the corporation will be most successful, and the share price is likely to remain the strongest, if all stakeholders continue to contribute to its success. Stakeholders are more likely to do so if their contributions are taken into account in corporate decision-making. Professor Stout wrote:

> ...The ideal rule for corporate directors to follow is not to require them to focus solely on maximizing shareholders' current wealth. Rather, the ideal rule of corporate governance, at least from an efficiency perspective, is to require corporate directors to maximize the sum of *all* the risk-adjusted returns enjoyed by *all* of the groups that participate in firms. These groups include not only shareholders, but also executives, employees, debtholders, and possibly even suppliers, consumers, and the broader community.[185]

Giving primacy to shareholders can have very negative impacts on other stakeholders. For example, the company may pay low wages, and lay off thousands of workers, in order to push up the price of the stock to benefit shareholders. Or the company may sell out to investors who offer the highest price per share but plan to dismantle the company, with devastating impacts on employees, families, and communities. Or the company may pollute the environment and harm local communities, in order to save money and increase shareholder value. Obviously, there are cases in which what is good for the shareholders is not good for other stakeholders or society at large.

As we will discuss below, the law does not require boards to give primacy to shareholders. Unfortunately, many board members don't know that, and may make unethical decisions as a result. Research conducted by Jacob Rose on corporate directors and social responsibility concluded that "directors favor shareholder value over personal ethical beliefs and social good because they believe that current corporate law requires them to pursue legal courses of action that maximize shareholder value."[186]

The participants in Rose's study were 34 active directors of U.S. *Fortune* 200 corporations, each of whom had served on an average of six boards and had an average of 20 years of management experience. The directors were divided into two groups—one group of 17 were asked to act as directors, and the second group of 17 was asked to act as partners in non-traded firms that did not have responsibilities to shareholders. Both groups were presented two case studies in which loopholes in the law would allow the corporation to cut down old-growth trees and emit a toxin at a high level that would threaten human health. In both cases, the unethical decision would increase earnings per share. Sixteen of the 17 directors voted to cut down the forest, and 15 of the 17 directors voted to emit the toxin and threaten human health, because doing so would improve earnings per share for shareholders. The results were different for the directors who were asked to take the perspective of partners without shareholders. Only 10 of the 17 directors voted to cut down the forest, and only 3 of the 17 voted to emit the toxin.[187] The belief in shareholder primacy was thus a major factor leading the directors to make unethical decisions that were harmful to the environment and to the health of human beings.

Recognizing other stakeholders and the public good

The need to recognize stakeholders other than shareholders was foreseen long ago. In 1932, Adolph Berle and Gardiner Means published their business classic, *The Modern Corporation & Private Property*. As they looked into the future, they could see a "third alternative" for corporate governance, beyond the choice between shareholders (whom they described as owners of passive property) and the control exercised by managers. They said:

> Neither the claims of ownership nor those of control can stand
> against the paramount interests of the community…It remains
> only for the claims of the community to be put forward with clarity

and force...Should the corporate leaders, for example, set forth a program comprising fair wages, security to employees, reasonable service to their public, and stabilization of business, all of which would divert a portion of the profits from the owners of passive property [the shareholders], and should the community generally accept such a scheme as a logical and human solution of industrial difficulties, the interests of passive property owners would have to give way. Courts would almost of necessity be forced to recognize the result...It is conceivable,—indeed, it seems almost essential if the corporate system is to survive,—that the 'control' of the great corporations should develop into a purely neutral technocracy, balancing a variety of claims by various groups in the community and assigning to each a portion of the income stream on the basis of public policy rather than private cupidity.[188]

Kent Greenfield, professor of law at the Boston College Law School, argued in *The Failure of Corporate Law* that it is time to revise corporate principles and policies. He said:

No corporation, even one making money for its core constituents, should be allowed to continue unchallenged and unchanged if its operation harms society...The corporation is an instrument whose purpose is to serve the collective good, broadly defined, and if it ceases to serve the collective good, it should not be allowed to continue its operation, at least not in the same way. If we knew that all corporations, or corporations of a certain type, or even an individual corporation created more social harm than good, no society in its right mind would grant incorporation to those firms.[189]

Greenfield said that the ultimate purpose of corporations should be to serve the interests of society as a whole, not just shareholders, and a corporation's wealth should be shared fairly among all those who contribute to its creation, not just shareholders.[190] Charters are granted to corporations for the public good, and the definition of public good needs to be broadened, as a matter of law and public policy.

In an article published in the *MIT Sloan Management Review*, Henry

Mintzberg, Robert Simons, and Kunal Basu criticized the "fabrication" that corporations exist to maximize shareholder value. They wrote:

> Corporations used to exist .. to serve society. Indeed, that was the reason they were originally granted charters—and why those charters could be revoked. Corporations are economic entities, to be sure, but they are also social institutions that must justify their existence by their overall contribution to society. Specifically, they must serve a balanced set of stakeholders...[191]

The Carver Policy Governance® Model

In the Carver Policy Governance® Model, boards take all stakeholders into account when they make decisions, but boards take them into account in different ways. Carver argues that the board owes an "ownership obligation" to shareholders and an "ethical obligation" to all other stakeholders. This resolves the shareholder primacy issue in a way that fulfills requirements for both performance and ethics. John Carver and Caroline Oliver stated:

> We assert that companies exist first and foremost for producing value for owners. In other words, an organization is *for* whatever its owners want it to be for...Therefore each board needs not only to be clear about who its owners are but to have some degree of dialogue with them before it can specify the kind of value their company should produce.. A company also has responsibilities to people other than owners...All obligations other than to provide value to owners are means issues rather than ends issues. Therefore a board will choose whatever degree of care it wishes with regard to stakeholders other than owners...[192]

Carver and Oliver acknowledged that the board will meet its legal obligations regarding public policies such as minimum wages and safety standards. The board will also recognize its responsibility to act ethically. Consumers, employees, and suppliers are to be treated with the proper respect. Finally, the corporation may make voluntary contributions to benefit society. "The company does not exist to fulfill such an obligation, but the board may still decide to make such contributions as a means of enhancing the company's long-term interests or fulfilling the board's interpretation of ethical social behavior."[193]

Considering all stakeholders can benefit shareholders

The argument that all stakeholders should be considered because that turns out to be best for shareholders, seems to be the position described in *The Corporate Director's Guidebook*, produced in 2007 by the American Bar Association (ABA) Committee on Corporate Laws. It stated:

> A number of state corporation statutes expressly allow the board to consider the interests of employees, suppliers, and customers, as well as the communities in which the corporation operates and the environment. Although the board may consider the interests of these other constituencies, the board is accountable primarily to shareholders for the performance of the corporation. Non-shareholder constituency considerations are best understood not as independent corporate objectives but as factors to be taken into account in pursuing the best interests of the corporation. Being responsive to stakeholder interests and concerns can help to contribute positively to a corporation's workplace culture as well as its reputation for integrity and ethical behavior.[194]

Considering the interests of other stakeholders may be in the best interests of the corporation, and therefore, presumably, in the best interests of shareholders.

While retaining the focus on shareholder primacy, the ABA Committee noted that the law is changing. Indeed, in most states today, the decisions of the board do not have to benefit shareholders. According to Micklethwait and Wooldridge, "during the 1980s, about half of America's fifty states introduced laws that allowed managers to consider other stakeholders alongside shareholders. Connecticut even introduced a law that required them to do so."[195]

The law supports director primacy

Professor Stout argued that, when given the choice between shareholder primacy and director primacy, most managers, shareholders, judges, and legislators choose *director* primacy. A study of the behavior of boards of directors conducted in 1989 by Jay Lorsch and Elizabeth MacIver found ambivalence about the shareholder primacy norm. The majority of directors saw themselves as accountable to more than one constituency.[196]

As for judges, the laws of Delaware are significant, since approximately half of all publicly traded companies are located in Delaware. "Delaware gives directors free rein to pursue strategies that reduce shareholder wealth while benefitting other constituencies," Stout noted.[197] An exception may occur when the directors seek to sell the company. In *Revlon, Inc. v. MacAndrews & Forbes Holdings, Inc.* the Delaware Supreme Court held that the board had a duty to maximize shareholder wealth by getting the best possible price, even if the impact of the sale would have negative impacts on other stakeholders.[198] However, state legislatures did not agree with the Delaware court. "Although Delaware pruned back *Revlon* by case law rather than by statute, in the wake of *Revlon*, over thirty other states have passed 'constituency' laws that expressly permit corporate directors to sacrifice shareholders' interests to serve other stakeholders."[199]

B Corporations and the Caux Roundtable

It is noteworthy that B Corporations (beneficial corporations) are now being established to address several problems, one of which is "the existence of shareholder primacy which makes it difficult for corporations to take employee, community, and environmental interests into consideration when making decisions."[200] The B Corporation legal framework expands the responsibilities of the corporation to include the stakeholder interests of their employees, communities, and the environment. The Declaration of Interdependence of B Corporations states:

> We envision a new sector of the economy which harnesses the power of private enterprise to create public benefit. This sector is comprised of a new type of corporation—the B Corporation—

which is purpose-driven and creates benefit for all stakeholders, not just shareholders. As members of this emerging sector and as entrepreneurs and investors in B Corporations, we hold these truths to be self-evident:

- That we must be the change we seek in the world.
- That all business ought to be conducted as if people and place mattered.
- That, through their products, practices, and profits, businesses should aspire to do no harm and benefit all.
- To do so requires that we act with the understanding that we are each dependent upon another and thus responsible for each other and future generations.[201]

Similar sentiments have been expressed by business leaders who developed the Caux Round Table's "Principles for Business," which are a worldwide vision for ethical and responsible corporate behavior. The three ethical foundations are responsible stewardship, living and working for mutual advantage, and the respect and protection of human dignity. The first of the seven principles is to "respect stakeholders beyond shareholders." This principle is elaborated as follows:

• A responsible business acknowledges its duty to contribute value to society through the wealth and employment it creates and the products and services it provides to consumers.
• A responsible business maintains its economic health and viability not just for shareholders, but also for other stakeholders.
• A responsible business respects the interests of, and acts with honesty and fairness towards, its customers, employees, suppliers, competitors, and the broader community.[202]

The Caux Roundtable has also established stakeholder management guidelines. In introducing the guidelines, the Caux Roundtable stated:

The key stakeholder constituencies are those who contribute to the success and sustainability of business enterprise. Customers provide cash flow by purchasing goods and services; employees produce the goods and services sold; owners and other investors provide funds for the business; suppliers provide vital resources; competitors provide efficient markets; communities provide social capital and operational security for the business; and the environment provides natural resources and other essential conditions.

In turn, key stakeholders are dependent on business for their well-being and prosperity. They are the beneficiaries of ethical business practices.[203]

While shareholder primacy has been a popular concept for decades, legislatures, courts, many business leaders, and even shareholders today understand what Greenleaf understood, that for-profit corporations have a public purpose, and their boards should take into account *all* the people that their organizations touch—employees, customers, business partners, and communities, as well as shareholders.

This page intentionally left blank

AN OVERVIEW OF SERVANT LEADERSHIP

In his classic essay, *The Servant as Leader*, Robert Greenleaf defined the servant-leader by saying:

> The servant-leader *is* servant first... It begins with the natural feeling that one wants to serve, to serve *first*. Then conscious choice brings one to aspire to lead. That person is sharply different from one who is *leader* first, perhaps because of the need to assuage an unusual power drive or to acquire material possessions...The leader-first and the servant-first are two extreme types. Between them there are shadings and blends that are part of the infinite variety of human nature.

> The difference manifests itself in the care taken by the servant-first to make sure that other people's highest priority needs are being served. The best test, and difficult to administer, is: Do those served grow as persons? Do they, *while being served*, become healthier, wiser, freer, more autonomous, more likely themselves to become servants? *And*, what is the effect on the least privileged in society? Will they benefit or at least not be further deprived?[204]

The term "servant-leader" joins two words that are often thought to be opposites—the servant, who is seen as fawning or obsequious, and the leader, who is seen as powerful and commanding. However, Greenleaf did not intend them to be equal or opposite. He said that "the servant-leader is servant first." He meant that "servant" is the fundamental, essential, true nature of the servant-leader. A servant-leader is therefore a person with a servant's heart who decides to lead.

Robert Greenleaf's concept of the servant-leader was stimulated by his reading of *Journey to the East* by Herman Hesse. It is the story of a group of travelers who were served by Leo, who did their menial chores. All went well until Leo disappeared one day. The travelers fell into disarray and could go no farther. The journey was over. Years later, one of the travelers saw Leo again—as the revered head of the Order that sponsored the journey. Leo, who had been their servant, was the titular head of the Order, a great and noble leader. In *The Servant as Leader,* Greenleaf said:

> …this story clearly says that *the great leader is seen as servant first,* and that simple fact is the key to his greatness. Leo was actually the leader all of the time, but he was servant first because that was what he was, *deep down inside.* Leadership was bestowed upon a man who was by nature a servant. It was something given, or assumed, that could be taken away. His servant nature was the real man, not bestowed, not assumed, and not to be taken away. He was servant first.[205]

Servant leadership grows out of servanthood. There are many ways to serve, and leading is one of them. When a person who is a servant at heart discovers the opportunity to make a difference by leading, and steps into a leadership role, then he or she becomes a servant-leader.

The single characteristic that distinguishes a servant-leader from other kinds of leader is thus the desire to serve, to be a servant *first.* A review of *The Servant as Leader* provides a fairly long list of characteristics that Greenleaf considered important in addition to the desire to serve. These might be considered techniques, skills, or attributes. They include listening and understanding; acceptance and empathy; foresight; awareness and perception; persuasion; conceptualization; self-healing; and rebuilding community. Greenleaf described servant-leaders as people who initiate action, are goal-oriented, are dreamers of great dreams, are good communicators, are able to withdraw and re-orient themselves, and are dependable, trusted, creative, intuitive, and situational.

Servant leadership has been supported by many leadership experts such as James Autry, Ken Blanchard, Stephen Covey, Peter Drucker, Max De Pree, Peter Senge, and Margaret Wheatley. They are drawn to servant leadership for a number of reasons, but all of them are supportive because servant leadership *works.*

Servant leadership works because of the specific practices of servant-leaders, practices that help them to be effective leaders and get positive results for their organizations. Seven of these key practices are self-awareness, listening, changing the pyramid, developing your colleagues, coaching not controlling, unleashing the energy and intelligence of others, and foresight. An explanation of these seven key practices can be found in *The Case for Servant Leadership*.[206] Here is a summary:

Self-Awareness

Each of us is the instrument through which we lead. If we want to be effective servant-leaders, we need to be aware of who we are and how we impact others. Other people are watching and reacting to our personalities, our strengths and weaknesses, our biases, our skills and experiences, and the way we talk and move and act. What we learn about ourselves depends on feedback from others and our own reflection—taking the time to think about how we behave, and why, and when, and consider whether there are other, better, more appropriate, more effective, more thoughtful ways to behave.

Listening

In *The Servant as Leader*, Greenleaf said that "only a true natural servant automatically responds to any problem by listening *first*."[207] Servant-leaders listen in as many ways as possible. They observe what people are doing. They conduct informal interviews, formal interviews, surveys, discussion groups, and focus groups. They use suggestions boxes. They do marketing studies and needs assessments. They are always asking, listening, watching, and thinking about what they learn. By listening, servant-leaders are able to identify the needs of their colleagues and customers. That puts them in a good position to *meet* those needs. When they do, their organizations are successful—their colleagues are able to perform at a high level, and they have happy customers, clients, patients, members, students, or citizens.

Changing the Pyramid

One of the obstacles to listening is the traditional organizational hierarchy—the pyramid. Often, members of the organization look up toward the top of the pyramid, and focus on pleasing their "bosses." But if everyone is looking up to please his or her boss, who is looking out, and paying attention to the needs of the customers? That's why servant-leaders talk about inverting the pyramid, or laying it on its side, so that everyone in the organization is focused on the people whom the organization is designed to serve.

Greenleaf pointed out that the person at the top of the pyramid has no colleagues, only subordinates. As a result, it is hard to get information, and it is hard to test new ideas. The chief may be the only person who doesn't know certain things, because nobody will tell him. Or people may share information that is biased, or incomplete, and they may not share the bad news, for fear that the chief will shoot the messenger. It is also hard for the chief to test ideas. People are reluctant to tell the chief that his or her idea is a bad one. The solution is obvious—servant-leaders create a team at the top. The team consists of senior leaders who are committed to the mission and to each other, who will share information, and who will challenge ideas. The chief is still the chief and makes final decisions, but those decisions will be far better informed and more relevant to the needs of those being served.

Developing Your Colleagues

Greenleaf proposed a new business ethic, which was that "*the work exists for the person as much as the person exists for the work*. Put another way, the business exists as much to provide meaningful work to the person as it exists to provide a product or service to the customer."[208] Work should provide people with opportunities to learn and grow and fulfill their potential. When your colleagues grow, the capacity of your organization grows. Developing colleagues includes a commitment to extensive on-the-job training, as well as formal education, new assignments, and internal promotions.

Coaching, not Controlling

Coaching and mentoring is a good way to develop people. Organizations need rules and regulations, but trying to control people doesn't bring out their best. Servant-leaders bring out the best in their colleagues by engaging, inspiring, coaching, and mentoring. Servant-leaders help their colleagues understand the organization's mission and their role in fulfilling it. Servant-leaders make sure their colleagues understand the organization's goals, and have the training and tools they need to achieve those goals.

Unleashing the Energy and Intelligence of Others

After developing and coaching their colleagues, servant-leaders unleash the energy and potential of their colleagues. People need experience making their own decisions, because occasions may arise when they need to be the leaders, or make a decision that they normally don't make. *Not* unleashing the energy and intelligence of others is extraordinarily sad and wasteful. It doesn't make any sense to have lots of people in an organization, but let only a few people—those at the top—use their full potential. Servant-leaders unleash everyone and encourage them to make the maximum contribution they can make to the organization and the people it serves.

Foresight

In *The Servant as Leader*, Greenleaf said that "prescience, or foresight, is a better than average guess about *what* is going to happen *when* in the future."[209] Greenleaf said that foresight is the "lead" that the leader has. A leader who is not out in front isn't really leading. He or she is only reacting. And a leader who is only reacting may run out of options, and get boxed in, and start making bad decisions—including unethical ones. Greenleaf said that foresight is the central ethic of leadership. The failure of a leader to foresee events may be viewed as an *ethical* failure, because a failure of foresight can put an organization in a bad situation that might have been avoided.

While there are other practices that help servant-leaders to be effective and successful, these seven are fundamental. They are about identifying and meeting the needs of others, so that colleagues can perform at their highest levels, and the organization can best serve its customers, clients, patients, members, students, or citizens. The key practices are about paying attention to people, developing people, and looking ahead so that servant-leaders and their colleagues will be able to continue serving others, far into the future.

Bibliography

American Bar Association Committee on Corporate Laws. *Corporate Director's Guidebook.* Chicago: ABA Publishing, 2007.

American Bar Association Committee on Corporate Laws. *Model Business Corporation Act.* Chicago: American Bar Foundation, 2003.

American Bar Association Committee on Nonprofit Corporations. *Guidebook for Directors of Nonprofit Corporations.* Chicago: ABA Publishing, 2002.

American Jurisprudence, 2nd Edition, Volume 18, Sec. 622. Thomson/West, 2004.

Bainbridge, Stephen M. *The New Corporate Governance in Theory and Practice.* Oxford: Oxford University Press, Inc., 2008.

Beatty, Jack, ed. *Colossus: How the Corporation Changed America.* New York: Broadway Books, 2001.

Berle, Adolph A. and Gardiner C. Means. *The Modern Corporation & Private Property.* New Brunswick, New Jersey: Transaction Publishers, 1991. [Originally published in 1932 by Harcourt, Brace & World, Inc.]

Blackwood, Amy, Kennard T. Wing and Thomas H. Pollak, *The Nonprofit Sector in Brief* [Facts and Figures from the Nonprofit Almanac 2008: Public Charities, Giving, and Volunteering]. Washington, D.C.: The Urban Institute, 2008.

BoardSource. *The Handbook of Nonprofit Governance*. San Francisco: Jossey-Bass, 2010.

BoardSource. *The Source: Twelve Principles of Governance that Power Exceptional Boards*. Washington, D.C.: BoardSource, 2005.

Broholm, Richard and Douglas Wysockey-Johnson. *A Balcony Perspective: Clarifying the Trustee Role*. St. Paul, Minnesota: Centered Life, 2004.

Bowen, William G. *The Board Book: An Insider's Guide for Directors and Trustees*. New York: W.W. Norton & Company, 2008.

Carver, John. *The Unique Double Servant Leadership Role of the Board Chairperson*. Westfield, Indiana: Greenleaf Center for Servant Leadership, 1999.

Carver, John and Miriam Mayhew Carver. *Basic Principles of Policy Governance*. San Francisco: Jossey-Bass, 1996.

Carver, John and Caroline Oliver. *Corporate Boards that Create Value: Governing Company Performance from the Boardroom*. San Francisco: Jossey-Bass, 2002.

Chait, Richard P., Thomas P. Holland, and Barbara E. Taylor. *The Effective Board of Trustees*. Westport, Connecticut: The Oryx Press, 1993 [American Council on Education Series on Higher Education].

Chait, Richard P., Thomas P. Holland, and Barbara E. Taylor. *Improving the Performance of Governing Boards*. Phoenix, Arizona: The Oryx Press, 1996. [American Council on Education Oryx Press Series on Higher Education].

Chait, Richard P., William P. Ryan, and Barbara E. Taylor. *Governance as Leadership: Reframing the Work of Nonprofit Boards*. Hoboken, New Jersey: John Wiley & Sons, 2005.

Charan, Ram. *Boards that Deliver: Advancing Corporate Governance from Compliance to Competitive Advantage*. San Francisco: Jossey-Bass, 2005.

Charan, Ram. *Boards at Work: How Corporate Boards Create Competitive Advantage.* San Francisco: Jossey-Bass, 1998.

DePree, Max. *Called to Serve: Creating and Nurturing the Effective Volunteer Board.* Grand Rapids, Michigan: William B. Eerdmans Publishing Company, 2001.

Dodge et al v. Ford Motor Co. et al, 170 N.W. 668 (Mich. 1919).

Drucker, Peter F. *Managing the Nonprofit Organization: Principles and Practices.* New York: Collins Business, 1990.

Drucker, Peter F. "Lessons for Successful Nonprofit Governance." *Nonprofit Management & Leadership*, Vol. 1, No. 1, Fall 1990, 7-13.

Frick, Don M. *Robert K. Greenleaf: A Life of Servant Leadership.* San Francisco: Berrett-Koehler Publishers, Inc., 2004.

Friedman, Milton. "The Social Responsibility of Business Is to Increase Its Profits." *The New York Times Magazine,* September 13, 1970.

Greenfield, Kent. *The Failure of Corporate Law: Fundamental Flaws and Progressive Possibilities.* Chicago: University of Chicago Press, 2006.

Greenleaf, Robert K. *Servant Leadership: A Journey into the Nature of Legitimate Power & Greatness.* New York: Paulist Press, 1977/2002.

Greenleaf, Robert K. *The Institution as Servant.* Westfield, Indiana: Greenleaf Center for Servant Leadership, 1972/2009.

Greenleaf, Robert K. *The Leadership Crisis.* Westfield, Indiana: Greenleaf Center for Servant Leadership, 1978.

Greenleaf, Robert K. *The Servant as Leader.* Westfield, Indiana: Greenleaf Center for Servant Leadership, 1970/2008.

Greenleaf, Robert K. *Trustees as Servants.* Westfield, Indiana: Greenleaf Center for Servant Leadership, 1974/2009.

Hartman, Thom. *Unequal Protection: The Rise of Corporate Dominance and the Theft of Human Rights.* San Francisco: Berrett–Koehler Publishers, Inc., 2002.

Heracleous, Loizos and Luh Luh Lan. "The Myth of Shareholder Capitalism." *Harvard Business Review*, April 2010, 1.

Ingram, Richard T. *Ten Basic Responsibilities of Nonprofit Boards.* Washington, D.C.: BoardSource, 2009.

Katzenbach, Jon R. and Douglas K. Smith. *The Wisdom of Teams: Creating the High-Performance Organization.* New York: Collins Business, 2003.

Keith, Kent M. *The Case for Servant Leadership.* Westfield, Indiana: The Greenleaf Center for Servant Leadership, 2008.

Michaelsen, Larry K., Warren E. Watson, and Robert H. Black. "A Realistic Test of Individual Versus Group Consensus Decision Making." *Journal of Applied Psychology*, 1989, Vol. 74, No. 5, 834-839.

Micklethwait, John and Adrian Wooldridge. *The Company: A Short History of a Revolutionary Idea.* New York: The Modern Library, 2005.

Mintzberg, Henry, Robert Simons, and Kunal Basu. "Beyond Selfishness." *MIT Sloan Management Review*, Fall 2002, Vol. 44, No. 1, 67-74.

Mokyr, Joel, ed. *The Oxford Encyclopedia of Economic History*, Vol. 2. Oxford: Oxford University Press, 2003.

Olson, James S., ed. *Encyclopedia of the Industrial Revolution in America.* Westport, Connecticut: Greenwood Press, 2002.

Parkinson, C. Northcote. *Parkinson's Law.* Boston: Houghton Mifflin Company, 1962.

Porter, Glenn, ed. *Encyclopedia of American Economic History.* New York: Charles Scribner's Sons, 1980.

Revlon, Inc. v. MacAndrews & Forbes Holdings, Inc., 506 A. 2d 173 (Del. 1986).

Rose, Jacob M. "Corporate Directors and Social Responsibility: Ethics versus Shareholder Value." *Journal of Business Ethics* (2007) 73: 319-331.

Shore, Bill. *The Cathedral Within.* New York: Random House, 1999.

Smith, David H. *Entrusted: The Moral Responsibilities of Trusteeship.* Indianapolis, Indiana: Indiana University Press, 1995.

Smith, D. Gordon. "The Shareholder Primacy Norm." *The Journal of Corporation Law*, Vol. 23, No. 2 [Winter 1998], 277-323.

Stout, Lynn A. "Bad and Not-So-Bad Arguments for Shareholder Primacy." *Southern California Law Review*, Vol. 75: 1189-1209 (2002).

Stout, Lynn A. "New Thinking on 'Shareholder Primacy.'" Working paper, August 26, 2010.

Taylor, Barbara E., Richard P. Chait, and Thomas P. Holland. "The New Work of the Nonprofit Board." *Harvard Business Review*, September-October 1996, pp. 4-11.

www.bcorporation.net

www.cauxroundtable.org

www.independentsector.org/economic_role

www.nationmaster.com/graph/eco_gro_nat_inc-economy-national-income

Yunus, Muhammad. *Creating a World Without Poverty.* New York: Public Affairs, 2007.

Notes

Preface

[1] Micklethwait and Wooldridge, *The Company*, xv.

[2] Ibid., 176.

[3] United States Department of State, cited at http://economics.about.com/od/smallbigbusiness/a/us_business.htm?p=1.

[4] Hartman, *Unequal Protection*, 37.

[5] www.nationmaster.com/graph/eco_gro_nat_inc-economy-gross-national-income.

[6] www.independentsector.org/economic_role, citing Kennard T. Wing, Thomas Pollak, and Amy Blackwood, *The Non-Profit Almanac 2008* (Washington, D.C.: The Urban Institute Press, 2008), 20.

[7] Blackwood, Wing and Pollak, *The Nonprofit Sector in Brief*, 1-2.

[8] Greenleaf, *The Servant as Leader*, 15.

[9] Many books and articles have been written about servant leadership since Greenleaf published his essays in the 1970s. See, for example, James A. Autry, *The Servant Leader: How to Build a Creative Team, Develop Great Morale, and Improve Bottom-Line Performance* (Roseville, California: Prima Publishing, 2001); James C. Hunter, *The Servant: A Simple Story About the True Essence of Leadership* (Rocklin, California: Prima Publishing, 1998); Kent M. Keith, *The Case for Servant Leadership* (Westfield, Indiana: The Greenleaf Center for Servant Leadership, 2008); Ken Blanchard, Scott Blanchard, and Drea Zigarmi, "Servant Leadership," Chapter 12 in Ken Blanchard and the Founding Associates and Consulting Partners of The Ken Blanchard Companies, *Leading at a Higher Level* (Upper Saddle River, New Jersey: Prentice Hall, 2007); Don M. Frick, *Implementing Servant Leadership: Stories from the Field* (La

Crosse, Wisconsin: Viterbo University, 2009); Ken Jennings and John Stahl-Wert, *The Serving Leader* (San Francisco: Berrett-Koehler Publishers, Inc., 2003); and James W. Sipe and Don M. Frick, *Seven Pillars of Servant Leadership* (New York: Paulist Press, 2009). For an overview of materials on servant leadership available as of 2008, see Betsy N. Hine, *The Hine Bibliography of Selected Monographic Resources on Servant Leadership* (Westfield, Indiana: The Greenleaf Center for Servant Leadership, 2008).

Chapter 1: Introduction

[10] Frick, *Robert K. Greenleaf: A Life of Servant Leadership*, 76.
[11] Greenleaf, *The Institution as Servant*, 9.
[12] Greenleaf, *Trustees as Servants*, 9.
[13] Ibid., 7.
[14] Ibid., 10.
[15] Ibid., 11.

Chapter 2: The Public Purpose of Corporations

[16] Berle and Means, *The Modern Corporation & Private Property*, 11.
[17] D. Gordon Smith, "The Shareholder Primacy Norm," 291.
[18] Ibid., 295.
[19] Beatty, *Colossus*, 51.
[20] Micklethwait and Wooldridge, *The Company*, 46.
[21] Hartman, *Unequal Protection*, 75.
[22] Micklethwait and Wooldridge, *The Company*, 45-46.
[23] Porter, *Encyclopedia of American Economic History*, 516; Mokyr, *The Oxford Encyclopedia of Economic History*, 319.
[24] Mokyr, *The Oxford Encyclopedia of Economic History*, 320.
[25] Adam Smith, often cited as the founder of modern economics, favored the owner-manager firm, instead of the joint stock company, which could only compete through the 'subsidy' of limited liability. Micklethwait and Wooldridge, *The Company*, 50.
[26] Ibid. Banks and other providers of credit during the early 19th century were reluctant to loan to a corporation unless the officers of the corporation personally endorsed the firm's notes, thus becoming personally liable for their repayment. Beatty, *Colossus*, 53.

[27] Olson, *Encyclopedia of the Industrial Revolution in America*, 57. Hartman argues that the U.S. Supreme Court, in the *Santa Clara County v. Union Pacific Railroad* decision in 1886, did not actually rule that corporations are persons, even though the case is known for that ruling. Instead, that statement that corporations are persons was written in the commentary on the case by the court reporter, J. C. Bancroft Davis, who was a lawyer, a former Acting Secretary of State for President Grant, and a champion of the rights of railroads. There were no statements in the actual ruling of the court to support Davis's commentary. Hartman, *Unequal Protection*, 116-119.

[28] Porter, *Encyclopedia of American Economic History*, 516, 521.

[29] Shore, *The Cathedral Within*, 124-143.

[30] Yunus, *Creating a World Without Poverty*, 21.

[31] Ibid., 21-22.

Chapter 3: Trustees for the Public Good

[32] Greenleaf, *Trustees as Servants*, 12.

[33] Ibid., 15.

[34] Heracleous and Lan reported: "…we conducted a systematic analysis of a century's worth of legal theory and precedent. It turns out that the law provides a surprisingly clear answer: Shareholders do not own the corporation, which is an autonomous legal person." Heracleous and Lan, "The Myth of Shareholder Capitalism," 1. See also the section of the Appendix on the shareholder primacy issue.

[35] *American Jurisprudence*, 457.

[36] Olson, *Encyclopedia of the Industrial Revolution in America*, 57.

[37] American Bar Association, *Guidebook for Directors of Nonprofit Corporations*, xviii.

[38] American Bar Association, *Model Business Corporation Act*, §8.01.

[39] American Bar Association, *Guidebook for Directors of Nonprofit Corporations*, xvii.

[40] Greenleaf, *Trustees as Servants*, 21.

[41] Ibid., 22.

[42] Ibid., 23.

[43] Ibid., 22.

[44] Ibid., 37.

[45] Bowen, *The Board Book*, 20.

[46] Bainbridge, *The New Corporate Governance*, 156.

[47] Chait, Holland and Taylor, *Improving the Performance of Governing Boards*, 59.

[48] Michaelsen, Watson, and Black, "Individual Versus Group Consensus Decision Making," 836.

[49] Bainbridge, *The New Corporate Governance*, 158-159.

[50] Drucker, "Lessons for Successful Nonprofit Governance," 9.

[51] Bainbridge, *The New Corporate Governance*, 160-161.

[52] Ibid., 177.

[53] Ibid.

[54] Ibid., 164 (quoting The Conference Board's *Corporate Governance Handbook*).

[55] Charan, *Boards that Deliver*, 3.

Chapter 4: The Role of the Board

[56] Bowen, *The Board Book*, 21.

[57] Carver, *Double Role of the Board Chairperson*, 6.

[58] Greenleaf, *Trustees as Servants*, 12-13.

[59] Bowen, *The Board Book*, 21-26.

[60] Ingram, *Ten Basic Responsibilities of Nonprofit Boards*, www.boardsource.org. See also Richard T. Ingram, *Ten Basic Responsibilities of Nonprofit Boards* (Washington, D.C.: BoardSource, 2009).

[61] Personal communication with Don Anderson, February 1, 2011.

[62] Drucker, *Managing the Nonprofit Organization*, 17.

[63] Greenleaf, *Trustees as Servants*, 34.

[64] Carver and Carver, *Basic Principles of Policy Governance*, 7.

[65] Ibid., 11.

[66] Ibid., 14.

[67] Smith, *Entrusted*, 5-16, 20.

[68] Chait, Ryan and Taylor, *Governance as Leadership*, 34.

[69] Ibid., 52.

[70] Ibid., 9.

[71] Ibid., 84.

[72] Ibid., 89.

[73] Greenleaf, *Trustees as Servants*, 41.

[74] Ibid., 42.

[75] Ibid., 43-44.

[76] BoardSource, *The Handbook of Nonprofit Governance*, 19.

[77] Greenleaf, *Trustees as Servants*, 36.

[78] Ibid., 35-36.

[79] De Pree, *Called to Serve*, 64.

[80] Ibid., 48-51.

[81] Chait, Holland, and Taylor, *Improving the Performance of Governing Boards*, 124-125.

[82] Greenleaf, *Trustees as Servants*, 35.

[83] Bowen, *The Board Book*, 61.

[84] Ibid., 46.

[85] Ibid., 49.

[86] Carver, *Double Role of the Board Chairperson*, 16-17.

[87] Ibid., 20.

Chapter 5: The Board and the Administration

[88] Greenleaf, *Trustees as Servants*, 14.

[89] Ibid., 13.

[90] Ibid., 14.

[91] Ibid.

[92] Taylor, Chait and Holland, "The New Work of the Nonprofit Board," 7.

[93] Ibid., 8.

[94] Ibid.

[95] Drucker, "Lessons for Successful Nonprofit Governance," 11.

[96] Bowen, *The Board Book*, 178-179.

[97] Smith, *Entrusted*, 112.

[98] BoardSource, *The Source: Twelve Principles*, 4.

[99] BoardSource, *The Handbook of Nonprofit Governance*, 40.

[100] Ibid.

[101] De Pree, *Called to Serve*, 84-88.

[102] Greenleaf, *Trustees as Servants*, 36.

[103] Carver and Carver, *Basic Principles of Policy Governance*, 5.

[104] Ibid., 4.

[105] Carver, *Double Role of the Board Chairperson*, 15.

[106] Ibid., 18.

[107] Drucker, "Lessons for Successful Nonprofit Governance," 10.

[108] Ibid.

[109] Greenleaf, *The Servant as Leader*, 15.

[110] Greenleaf, *Trustees as Servants*, 18.

[111] Taylor, Chait, and Holland, "The New Work of the Nonprofit Board," 5.

[112] Broholm and Wysockey-Johnson, *A Balcony Perspective*, 19.

[113] Ibid., 20.

[114] Greenleaf, *Trustees as Servants*, 34.

[115] Charan, *Boards that Deliver*, 129.

[116] Greenleaf, *Trustees as Servants*, 23.

[117] Ibid., 24.

[118] Ibid.

[119] Ibid., 25.

[120] Bowen, *The Board Book*, 22.

[121] Charan, *Boards at Work*, xix.

[122] Bowen, *The Board Book*, 3.

Chapter 6: The Effective Board

[123] Greenleaf, *Trustees as Servants*, 32-33.

[124] Katzenbach and Smith, *The Wisdom of Teams*, 21.

[125] Ibid., 9.

[126] Ibid., 19.

[127] Ibid., 18-19.

[128] Greenleaf, *Trustees as Servants*, 45.

[129] Chait, Holland and Taylor, *Improving the Performance of Governing Boards*, 59.

[130] BoardSource, *The Handbook of Nonprofit Governance*, 15.

[131] Carver and Carver, *Basic Principles of Policy Governance*, 2.

[132] Ibid., 3-4.

[133] Carver, *Double Role of the Board Chairperson*, 13.

[134] Chait, Holland and Taylor, *The Effective Board of Trustees*, 2.

[135] Ibid.

[136] Ibid., 3.

[137] Ibid.

[138] Ibid.

[139] Ibid.

[140] Chait, Holland and Taylor, *Improving the Performance of Governing Boards*, 1.

[141] Ibid., 9.

[142] Ibid., 9-16.

[143] Taylor, Chait, and Holland, "The New Work of the Nonprofit Board," 4.

[144] Ibid.

[145] De Pree, *Called to Serve*, 32.

[146] Ibid., 18.

[147] Carver and Carver, *Basic Principles of Policy Governance*, 6-11.

[148] Parkinson, *Parkinson's Law*, 24.

[149] Greenleaf, *Trustees as Servants*, 18.

[150] Charan, *Boards that Deliver*, 21.

[151] BoardSource, *The Source: Twelve Principles*, 10-11.

[152] Charan, *Boards that Deliver*, 21.

[153] Ibid., 48-49.

[154] Greenleaf, *The Servant as Leader*, 18.

[155] De Pree, *Called to Serve*, 14.

[156] Greenleaf, *The Servant as Leader*, 25.

[157] Greenleaf, *Trustees as Servants*, 18.

[158] Ibid., 45-47.

[159] Chait, Holland and Taylor, *Improving the Performance of Governing Boards*, 1.

[160] Ibid., 1-2.

[161] De Pree, *Called to Serve*, 73.

[162] BoardSource, *The Source: Twelve Principles*, 13.

[163] Taylor, Chait and Holland, "The New Work of the Nonprofit Board," 10.

[164] Bowen, *The Board Book*, 136.

[165] Greenleaf, *The Servant as Leader*, 45-46.

[166] Greenleaf, *The Leadership Crisis*, 8-9.

Chapter 7: The Call to Serve

[167] Greenleaf, *Trustees as Servants*, 51-52.

Appendix: The Shareholder Primacy Issue

[168] Ibid., 15.

[169] Stout, "New Thinking on 'Shareholder Primacy,'" 2.

[170] Smith, "The Shareholder Primacy Norm," 278.

[171] *Dodge v. Ford Motor Company*, 684.

[172] Ibid., 671.

[173] *American Jurisprudence*, 169-171.

[174] Smith, "The Shareholder Primacy Norm," 279.

[175] Ibid.

[176] Ibid., 286.

[177] Stout, "New Thinking on 'Shareholder Primacy,'" 3.

[178] Milton Friedman, "The Social Responsibility of Business Is to Increase Its Profits."

[179] Ibid.

[180] Stout, "Bad and Not-So-Bad Arguments for Shareholder Primacy," 1191.

[181] Ibid., 1194.

[182] Stout, "New Thinking on 'Shareholder Primacy,'" 9.

[183] Ibid., 10.

[184] Stout, "Bad and Not-So-Bad Arguments for Shareholder Primacy," 1207.

[185] Ibid., 1198.

[186] Rose, "Corporate Directors and Social Responsibility," 320.

[187] Ibid., 325.

[188] Berle and Means, *The Modern Corporation & Private Property*, 312-313.

[189] Greenfield, *The Failure of Corporate Law*, 127.

[190] Ibid., 142.

[191] Mintzberg, Simons, and Basu, "Beyond Selfishness," 69-70.

[192] Carver and Oliver, *Corporate Boards that Create Value*, 60-61.

[193] Ibid., 62.

[194] American Bar Association, *Corporate Director's Guidebook*, 13.

[195] Micklethwait and Wooldridge, *The Company*, 150.

[196] Smith, "The Shareholder Primacy Norm," 291.

[197] Stout, "Bad and Not-So-Bad Arguments for Shareholder Primacy," 1202.

[198] *Revlon*, 506 A. 2d at 185.

[199] Stout, "Bad and Not-So-Bad Arguments for Shareholder Primacy," 1204.

[200] www.bcorporation.net.

[201] Ibid.

[202] www.cauxroundtable.org

[203] Ibid.

Appendix: An Overview of Servant Leadership

[204] Greenleaf, *The Servant as Leader*, 15.

[205] Ibid., 9.

[206] Keith, *The Case for Servant Leadership*, 31-55.

[207] Greenleaf, *The Servant as Leader*, 18.

[208] Greenleaf, *Servant Leadership*, 154-155.
[209] Greenleaf, *The Servant as Leader*, 25.

Acknowledgments

I would like to thank those who commented on the book while it was being written: Phil Anderson, Jeff Blade, Richard Broholm, John Carver, Jim Emrich, Dolores Jones, Courtney Knies, Isabel Lopez, Dr. Ann McGee-Cooper, Rob Parker, Robert Phipps, Richard R. Pieper, Sr., Barry Schneider, and Dr. Robert Thomas. I am grateful for the gift of their time and insight, which made the book a better book. Any errors or misunderstandings are my responsibility alone.

About the Author

Dr. Kent M. Keith is the Chief Executive Officer of the Greenleaf Center for Servant Leadership. He has been an attorney, a state government official, a high tech park developer, a university president, a YMCA executive, and a full-time speaker and author. He has served on several dozen boards in the public, private, and non-profit sectors.

Dr. Keith earned a B.A. in Government from Harvard University, an M.A. in Philosophy and Politics from Oxford University, a Certificate in Japanese from Waseda University, a J.D. from the University of Hawaii, and an Ed.D. from the University of Southern California. He is a Rhodes Scholar.

Dr. Keith is known internationally as the author of the Paradoxical Commandments, which he first published in 1968 in a booklet for student leaders. He is the author of four books about the commandments, including *Anyway: The Paradoxical Commandments*, which became a national bestseller and was translated into 17 languages. He is also the author of *The Case for Servant Leadership*, published by the Greenleaf Center.

Over the years, Dr. Keith has given more than 1,000 conference papers, presentations, and seminars. He has been featured on the front page of *The New York Times* and in *People* magazine, *The Washington Post*, *The San Francisco Chronicle*, and *Family Circle*, and has been quoted in *The Wall Street Journal* and *Inc.com*. He has appeared on dozens of TV shows and more than 100 radio programs in the United States, the United Kingdom, Japan, Korea, and Australia. More information about Dr. Keith can be found at www.kentmkeith.com.

About the Greenleaf Center

The Greenleaf Center for Servant leadership was founded by Robert K. Greenleaf, who launched the modern servant leadership movement in 1970 with the publication of his classic essay, *The Servant as Leader*. The Greenleaf Center is an international non-profit organization whose mission is to promote the awareness, understanding, and practice of servant leadership by individuals and organizations.

The Center publishes and sells books and essays, and hosts an international conference, a healthcare conference, a Leadership Institute for Educators, and regional conferences. The Center provides keynote speakers on servant leadership for special events, as well as half-day and full-day Greenleaf Seminars. The Greenleaf Academy offers a certificate program, and the Greenleaf Scholars Program grants scholarships for doctoral-level research on the impacts of servant leadership. For more information about the Center, please contact:

The Greenleaf Center for Servant Leadership
133 Peachtree St. NE
Lobby Suite 350
Atlanta, GA 30303
www.greenleaf.org

Servant Leadership Publications

The following publications are among many that are available from the Greenleaf Center for Servant Leadership online at www.greenleaf.org/ catalog or by calling the Center at 317-669-8050.

Servant Leadership: A Journey into the Nature of Legitimate Power and Greatness (25th Anniversay Edition) by Robert K. Greenleaf. This is the first collection of Greenleaf's major essays on servant leadership, originally published in 1977. The collection includes his first three major essays, *The Servant as Leader, The Institution as Servant,* and *Trustees as Servants.* The 25th anniversary edition features a Foreword by Stephen R. Covey and an Afterword by Peter M. Senge. ($23.00)

The Servant as Leader by Robert K. Greenleaf. This is the essay that launched the modern servant leadership movement in the 1970s. Greenleaf tells the story of Leo; defines the servant-leader; and discusses the importance of listening, empathy, awareness, foresight, persuasion, and conceptualization. Hundreds of thousands of copies of this essay have been sold throughout the world, and it has been translated into more than a dozen languages. ($9.00 per copy. Quantity discounts are available.)

The Institution as Servant by Robert K. Greenleaf. Greenleaf's second major essay challenges conventional wisdom about hierarchical organizational structures and the use of power in major institutions. He presents new models for implementing servant leadership in organizations. ($9.00 per copy. Quantity discounts are available.)

Trustees as Servants by Robert K. Greenleaf. Greenleaf's third essay addresses the importance of trustees (board members), the uniqueness of board judgments, and the need to clarify and strengthen the trustee role. ($9.00 per copy. Quantity discounts are available.)

The Unique Double Servant Leadership Role of the Board Chairperson by John Carver. This paper, presented at the Greenleaf Center's 1998 International Conference, describes the role of the board as a group servant-leader, and the role of the chair as servant-leader to the board. The paper explains the role of the chair as construed by the Policy Governance® Model developed by Carver. ($9.00 per copy. Quantity discounts are available.)

The Case for Servant Leadership by Kent M. Keith. This book is an introduction to servant leadership, including the writings of Robert K. Greenleaf and others in the servant leadership movement. It defines servant leadership, and explains the ways in which it is ethical, practical, and meaningful. The book includes questions for reflection and discussion. ($12.00 per copy. Quantity discounts are available.)

Servant-Institutions in Business by Jerry Glashagel. This book tells how eight companies approach the challenge of serving their employees, customers, business partners and communities, and outlines the characteristics of servant-institutions in business. ($12.00 per copy. Quantity discounts are available.)

Start with Humility: Lessons from America's Quiet CEOs on How to Build Trust and Inspire Followers by Merwyn A. Hayes and Michael D. Comer. The book discusses the true meaning of humility; why humility is a key to successful leadership; and the characteristics of leaders who start with humility. It features the stories of five individuals who have succeeded as humble leaders. Each chapter includes leadership lessons, a leadership self-assessment, and leadership actions that the reader can write down and implement. ($15.00 per copy. Quantity discounts are available.)

Made in the USA
Monee, IL
11 October 2021

79485498R00073